The Book of...
Relationship
Building

Understanding People, Building Rapport, and Creating Meaningful Connections

Scott D. Snell

losses, direct or indirect, that are incurred as a result of the use of the information contained within this document, including, but not limited to, errors, omissions, or inaccuracies.

Table of Contents

Preface

Scott Snell

Book 1 – The Book of… Relationship Building

Ever since I was a teenager, I have been interested in relationships, how people interact, and how friendships are built and broken. What makes someone tick and act how they do? During college, I studied sociology, and at university, I studied business and marketing, and my interest in the importance of human connections and people continued to grow.

I have spent over 25 years working with people, working for people, building relationships with customers, and leading people. I have worked for some major corporations and worked with some of the biggest customers in the world. What is consistent across all aspects of my life is the need to build connections. Whether you are raising children, securing a large-scale business deal, making a complaint, or working within a team, it is our relationships that make the difference.

A lot is written about technology and, most recently, AI and how machines will replace humans... I challenge this, and my experience is that when it comes down to it, the relationships we have with ourselves and with the people around us are key to our well-being and leading a fulfilling life. I am looking to share my experiences to help you.

This is not an academic book; it is intended to be a practical guide to help you understand your role in relationships, how you can build better relationships, and the impact it could have on your happiness and well-being. I am not looking to confuse you with in-depth research on relationships but to give you simple and practical guidance.

I have a vision of developing a series of books to help people lead better lives, be better to work with, work for, manage, lead, and hopefully help fulfill their potential. The series will share simple ways of unlocking your potential, including authenticity, inclusivity, resilience...

Enjoy the journey, and I hope you find one or two things that will make a difference to you and the relationships you have with others.

Introduction

Relationships are tricky things. On the one hand, they're something even the most introverted want. We want to have close relationships with our friends and families. We want to forge strong and healthy romantic relationships that will last years. We want to form cordial and respectful bonds with our colleagues and superiors to work in harmony and get things done.

On the other hand, forming such relationships can be difficult. Meeting new people, for instance, can be incredibly stressful, to the point that you have no idea what to say or how to start. Conversation can become stalled, leading you to experience the dreaded awkward pause. Sometimes, you'll find you are not as close to someone as you originally thought. Other times, you might be at a loss about how to grow closer to someone. At others still, you might find yourself dealing with the frustration of misunderstandings and miscommunication.

The good news is you're not alone in these experiences, just as you're not alone in wanting to form close relationships with others. We all want close relationships, yet we struggle with forming, maintaining, and strengthening them. Odds are, we will continue to do so until the end of time. That's not necessarily a bad thing, though. Like anything that's of value in this world, relationships take work. If you care about something or someone, you'll be willing to put in the hard work necessary to build a good relationship with them. You'll be willing to overcome the various roadblocks you may encounter along the way, too, because you'll know it will be worth it.

The key to doing all of this is communication, which is both a very powerful tool and one that can be difficult. On the surface, communication seems pretty easy. After all, we communicate with people every day, be it writing, over the phone, or face-to-face. If you've ever experienced a misunderstanding or found yourself in an argument where you end up saying something you don't mean, you know that that's not the case. You also know that poor communication can damage your relationships, be it with a loved one or a colleague at work. Yet, you also know that, when used correctly, communication can be a game changer in many respects. That's why, over the years and centuries, it has proven to be the cornerstone of human civilization and development. Communication has been vital to the very survival of humankind. That's why it was invented: so information that's essential to the survival of other individuals and groups can be relayed to them.

Imagine that you're living in the Stone Age and know for a fact that a particular berry that grows near the caves you and your tribe live in is poisonous. One bite is enough to kill a grown man. As you're walking by, your tribe comes across the berries, and a number of the tribe members head toward them, intending to eat them. If you want them to survive—and I imagine that you do—you need to communicate the information you have, thereby preventing them from devouring the berries and, thus, ending their lives. Communication was born out of the need to communicate this type of information. These days, it serves a much greater purpose.

While communication still helps us impart life-saving information, particularly if you happen to be a doctor, it achieves so much more. Aside from helping you strengthen your relationships, it makes it possible for you to work toward shared goals—something that colleagues and classmates have to do often, no matter how little they know one another.

Say you've been given a large project at work or school. You can't do everything alone, so you must work with others. To do so, you must communicate with your colleagues and decide who's responsible for what. You need to make sure everyone understands their responsibilities and set clear timelines for when each of their tasks and the overall project needs to be completed. You need to have a check system in place to make sure everything is going smoothly. Should any problems arise, you need to be able to discuss them among yourselves openly and find a solution for them together. You can do all of that only if you can clearly communicate with your colleagues.

Luckily, communication is also an innate skill for humans in many ways. We are hardwired to be social beings or pack animals. We have evolved to crave human connection and communication. As we've seen, this evolution was vital for our survival. In the past, having good relationships with others meant having people willing to share food and water with you in times of scarcity. There's ample evidence from millions of years ago—about 1.8 to 2.6 million, to be specific—that showed human beings used to collect food from multiple locations and then bring it to a communal eating space to share with others, making sure no one went hungry in the process (*Human Characteristics: Social Life*, 2022). Being a pack animal also meant having someone to help raise your young, offer you shelter when needed, and impart important survival information—like which berries were poisonous and where predators lurked.

Our instincts to build relationships and communicate with others come from this primal age where everyone had to rely on each other to live. These instincts are still alive within us today. Consider how you act around people you like. You often have an instinct to reach out and touch them. This can mean giving them a pat on the back, brushing their hair out of their face, clapping them on the shoulder, holding their hand... Such actions aren't things you consciously think about doing. You do them simply because your instincts tell you to. In doing so, you communicate your love, care, and appreciation for them since—contrary to what some might think—communication isn't solely verbal. In fact, between 80% and 90% of all communication is nonverbal among human beings (Thompson, 2011). That means you communicate a massive amount of information, such as your thoughts and feelings, to others without saying much.

Communicating positive thoughts and feelings nonverbally to the people in your life, especially those you care about, has a ripple effect. This is because emotions are contagious. You can easily catch another person's emotion when it's reflected to you through nonverbal communication. This is because of a neural phenomenon called neuroplasticity (Kong, 2022). It works like this: You observe someone displaying a certain emotion, let's say it's fear, through their body language. This gives your brain the message, "There's something we need to be afraid of." Your brain's alarm system is triggered, and you look for potential threats. You pick up the fear the person before you is feeling, even if you personally have nothing to fear.

If you're skeptical about this, remember the last time you watched a scary horror movie. How did you react to it on a physical level? Odds are your heart started pounding, your breathing pace picked up, your palms began sweating... In other words, you started showing all the physiological signs of fear. Yet, you had nothing to be afraid of, at least not really. The threat you were watching was fictional. Now, the fact that someone's body language, facial expressions, and words can impact you in such a visceral way means that yours can affect others in just the same manner. It's important to be aware of this fact because when you are, you can use your various communication methods, such as your body language, to relay the right feelings, sentiments, thoughts, and information to others. In the process, you get to spread the love, so to speak, exchange more useful information with others, foster stronger connections, and attain greater awareness and knowledge of the world around you. All in all, you get to build stronger relationships with your friends and family and at work. You get to build friendships you truly value; start the kind of loving, supportive family you want; and become the success you aim to be at work.

All of this and more is possible when you have strong relationships with others. However, building those relationships takes time and effort. It requires spending that time and effort on your interpersonal relationships but also yourself. Think of it this way: Why would others show you love, care, and respect in their relationships with you if you cannot show love, care, and respect to yourself? People take their cues on how to treat others from the very people they're dealing with. So, if you want people to treat you in a certain way and build a relationship, you need to start treating yourself that way as well. This can be hard for some people, just as mastering clear, positive communication can be challenging. Hard and challenging don't automatically translate to impossible, though—at least not when you know what to do to overcome the hurdles before you.

Overcoming those hurdles, especially within the workplace, is just one of the things you will learn how to do in *The Book of... Relationships*. You will not only discover how to master positive verbal and nonverbal communication but also how to form strong, loving, and trusting relationships with others and with yourself. In doing so, you'll obtain the tools you need to create the kind of life, family, and work environment you want. You'll discover what you need to do to change things in the way that you want. By the time you reach the end of this book, you will have all you need to slowly but surely begin the transformative process that will turn you from an introverted caterpillar, if that is indeed what you are, to a social butterfly able to communicate with your colleagues, superiors, and those who are under your management easily and effectively.

Having said that, there is one thing you need to understand before you can begin this process, and that's what a healthy relationship looks like, be it with others or yourself. How can you start building strong, healthy relationships if you have no idea how they're supposed to work? How can you start cultivating them if you don't know the ingredients you need? With all this in mind, let's turn the page to properly begin our journey and dive into the world of health relationships. Let's discover what such a relationship is and isn't.

Chapter 1:

What Makes a Healthy

Relationship?

Relationships come in all shapes and sizes. There are romantic relationships and friendships, close acquaintance-ships and employee-employer relationships, and the bonds you form with your parents and kids. All these relationships are a vital part of your life but are all inherently different. Consider your friendships. It's an undeniable fact that you are closer to some people than you are to others. Your relationship with your work friend, with whom you always grab lunch, is very different from your relationship with your best friend, and it should be. Similarly, your relationship with your best friend differs from that with your manager at work or acquaintance-ship with the person in the cubicle next to you. Assuming your cubicle neighbor isn't your best friend, that's how it should be.

As different as these relationships may be, though, you can typically divide them into one of two categories: healthy relationships and toxic ones. As a rule, you want to form healthy relationships with others and avoid toxic ones. A healthy relationship is built on mutual trust, honesty, openness, and respect—the key tenets of any type of relationship. Speaking of keys, the keyword there is "mutual." A toxic relationship decidedly lacks such tenets. It's the kind of relationship that makes you feel unsupported, misunderstood, demeaned, and maybe even attacked (Scott, 2020). As you can surmise, a healthy relationship makes you feel good. A toxic relationship makes you feel bad.

That's not to say that a healthy relationship will always make you feel happy. No relationship can ever make you feel happy all the time because happiness is, by its nature, fleeting. This is true of every emotion we human beings are capable of having, be it positive or negative. So, expecting perpetual happiness when you get into, say, a romantic relationship is rather unfair. It puts too much pressure on that relationship, and it is impossible to meet expectations. This is something that people who have such expectations usually fail to realize. As such, they find that they are disappointed in their relationship. Not only that but thinking that their relationship must be a failure since it's not making them happy all the time, they usually give up on it and end things. They then go off to search for the "perfect" relationship they're looking for, not realizing that what they envision isn't possible to achieve.

So, if the mark of a healthy relationship isn't that it makes us happy all the time, what is? How can you tell a healthy relationship from a toxic one? How do you even begin to define and build a healthy relationship? Let's find out.

A Healthy Relationship? What's That?

Having good, healthy relationships in your life is imperative for both your happiness and well-being. You might think that's an exaggeration, but studies prove as much. According to one, having healthy relationships makes you more likely to develop and stick with healthy habits. This same study has shown that people who have healthy relationships tend to be physically healthier as a result (Antonucci et al., 2014). Another similar study has shown that people who have healthy relationships actually live longer lives than people who don't (Yang et al., 2016).

If you're wondering why all this is the case, the answer has to do with stress. You see, having strong, healthy relationships is something that lowers the stress and anxiety you experience in your day-to-day life. Stress, or at least chronic stress, can impact your health in some pretty drastic ways. For one, it can keep your heart rate constantly elevated, thereby tiring out your heart and cardiovascular system (*The Health Benefits of Strong Relationships*, 2010). This can lead to a myriad of cardiovascular diseases, including heart attacks. For another, the hormones that flood your system impact your immune system negatively and can weaken it. This makes it easier for you to get sick and makes it harder for you to recover from a disease. None of these things are good for your overall health and longevity. It's a good thing, then, that healthy social relationships trigger the release of stress-reducing hormones in your body, preventing you from experiencing such things. This goes double for any time someone you have a social relationship with offers you some form of support.

Good social support is one of the cornerstones and defining features of healthy relationships. Of course, receiving support from someone means being able to trust them enough to ask for support. This is why trust is one of the cornerstones of healthy relationships (Cherry, 2023). When you form a healthy relationship with someone, you can trust them with your troubles, insecurities, and worries. You trust that they won't make fun of you for these things or take advantage of them. You trust that they won't judge you for these things and can ask for help or support from them when you need it. So, if you have a healthy relationship with your manager, for instance, you should be able to ask for their support when you're having a tough time at work. Signs that you have a trusting relationship with someone are that the two of you treat one another well and you consider one another dependable. You feel comfortable sharing things with them, even your perceived weaknesses, and feel you can rely on their support. Not only that, but you know they feel the same way and can come to you with their vulnerabilities.

Healthy relationships are also characterized by openness and honesty. Now, this doesn't mean you have to have the same level of openness with everyone in your life. You may have a healthy relationship with your work friends, but you wouldn't be as open with them about your marital troubles as you would with your siblings or close friends. That's perfectly normal and understandable since different relationships have different boundaries—something that healthy relationships need, as you'll see momentarily. Still, even at these varying levels, healthy relationships require being honest and open about yourself. They require honest self-disclosure. In other words, they require that you share things about yourself with others—your true thoughts, feelings, experiences, interests, and beliefs, to give a few examples.

Openness and honesty are necessary parts of healthy relationships because they establish and strengthen trust. At the same time, they make you feel more connected to the person you're talking to. Again, though, having a healthy relationship with someone doesn't mean sharing everything with them. There is such a thing as boundaries, after all. A lot of people seem to think that boundaries are a bad thing. They think that having boundaries implies a lack of trust. The truth is the exact opposite. This is because boundaries aren't about keeping secrets and hiding things. They're about establishing your needs and expectations so they can be met. They're about trust because when you set a boundary with someone, you trust that they will respect it. If they do, it makes you feel safe. Later on, as you grow closer, you may decide to move that boundary, or you may not. It's entirely up to you.

Another mark of a healthy relationship is respect. A relationship where someone is constantly belittling the other isn't a respectful one. It's not a healthy one because a lack of respect means a lack of good communication and trust. Why would you trust someone with your innermost feelings if you know you'll be mocked for it? Why would you share something with a work friend or confide in your manager that you are having a tough time if you worry they'll belittle you for it, however subtly? Now, respect can be conveyed in any number of ways in a relationship. Actively listening to the person and paying attention to their words is one way. Another is building them up instead of making them feel small. Taking an interest in the things they enjoy, being understanding if and when they make a mistake, and showing your gratitude or appreciation for them are other examples of respectful behaviors in healthy relationships.

Perhaps the biggest sign of a healthy relationship, though, is give and take. There are times in our lives when we need extra support. It's important to ask for help in these times, and the people with whom we have healthy relationships will typically readily give us that help. They will also be able to confidently turn to us to ask for help when they need it. This is a prime example of reciprocity—otherwise known as give and take—which is the mark of a healthy relationship. Good relationships are two-sided. You are there for others just as much as they are there for you. You spend as much time, energy, and effort on others as they spend on you. If you're in a relationship where you are always the one giving and never or seldom the one receiving anything—be it time, support, or something else—then that is an imbalanced relationship and, therefore, an unhealthy one. It must be stated again, though, that this is true of relationships in general. It does not apply to those moments when you're going through something, like a loss, and need more support and are unable to show support to others at that time.

Relationship Red Flags

Just as healthy relationships have certain set characteristics—or green flags—so do unhealthy or toxic relationships. A toxic relationship makes you feel alone, unsupported, misunderstood, and sometimes even attacked. Being in such a relationship can be a very debilitating and isolating experience. It can whittle away at your sense of self, as well as your self-confidence. If you're in such a relationship for too long, it can lead to an array of mental health disorders, including depression. To be clear, a toxic relationship isn't necessarily an abusive one. Abusive relationships, however, are always toxic, and toxic relationships can evolve into abusive ones over time.

The reason this can happen is simple: At its core, a toxic relationship is built on a lack of respect, especially for the boundaries a person sets for themselves. A lack of boundaries or a lack of respect for boundaries is a key sign that you're in a toxic relationship (Scott, 2020). Say that one of your boundaries is that you don't want to receive work calls after work hours, assuming it's not a vital emergency. This is a perfectly reasonable boundary to have. However, your manager doesn't agree. The first time your manager called you after work, you got mad but ultimately let it go. It was just the one time, you reasoned. Then, it happened again, this time on a weekend, and you tried to explain why this wasn't acceptable to you. Your manager seemed to agree, but a little while later, the same thing happened again, then again, and again, with no signs of stopping.

Now, the first time your manager does this might be something you could forgive. After all, you might reason they didn't realize this was a boundary for you and they may have genuinely thought they were dealing with an emergency. The second time, you got mad but could let it go because your manager could have just forgotten. The third time, though? Your manager can't claim to have forgotten your boundary again, which means that they chose to violate it willingly. When you got upset this time, they got upset back, claiming that your boundary was a clear sign that you didn't value your job. In other words, instead of respecting your boundary, they both violated it and tried to justify their actions. Both these things connote a clear lack of respect for your needs. They also imply a lack of trust, which is why the willful crossing of boundaries is a major red flag in any relationship, and so is a lack of trust.

Healthy relationships are supposed to bring out the best in you. So, one sign that you're not in a healthy relationship is that it brings out the worst in you. Say you have a work friend. Ordinarily, you're a straightforward person. When you and this friend get together, though, you tend to gossip about everyone else at the office behind their backs. In the process, you say some very hurtful things about people you're supposedly close to. Odds are, you're not the only person who does this with this friend. They likely talk behind your back with your other colleagues, too. That you fall into this kind of pattern with this friend doesn't sound very healthy and neither does the uncomfortable truth that you can never fully trust such a work friend.

They could be saying anything about you when you're not there, after all.

One very definitive sign that you're in an unhealthy relationship is that you always feel like you have to walk on eggshells around the person you're dealing with. If you've ever had a boss who has made you feel like this, you know exactly what that's like. Such a boss can accuse you of any number of things, like not caring about your work or intentionally doing things to hurt the company or projects you're working on. Anytime something goes wrong, you are the one who takes the blame, even when, objectively speaking, you did nothing wrong. In the aftermath of arguments, you are the one who's always apologizing. Responsibility never lies with them, only with you.

A final sign that you are in an unhealthy relationship is becoming someone's perpetual cheerleader. Don't get me wrong; there will times in any relationship where you spend time and effort trying to uplift someone else's feelings. The problem arises when you have to do this constantly. Being someone's constant cheerleader can be a very draining experience. It can result in you spending a ridiculous amount of time on someone else and neglecting your own needs, emotional or otherwise, in the process. In other words, it can result in you feeling completely unsupported.

There's even an officially recognized term for relationships featuring this type of behavior: codependent. Codependency is a dangerous state to find yourself in. In this state, you essentially become emotionally dependent or addicted to someone else (Gould, 2020). Because you become addicted to them, you start doing anything and everything you can to keep them content. So, you start walking on eggshells. You let them cross whatever boundaries you have. You prioritize their needs and wants above your own all the time. You feel the need to get their permission whenever you want to do something for yourself. You are always the one apologizing, no matter what has gone wrong, regardless of whether you were at fault or not. You always try to fix things for them and become willing to do anything for them. In the end, you completely lose your sense of self, to the point where you don't know who you are anymore.

You might have noticed that codependency features all the common marks of toxic relationships. This is because codependent relationships are a form of unhealthy relationships. There are different forms of toxic relationships, and understandably, none of them lead to happiness. In this sense, it's a bit like what Tolstoy said, "All happy families are alike; each unhappy family is unhappy in its own way," except you have to switch out the word "family" with the word "relationship" (Tolstoy, 1877/2008). As you can guess, that means that there are simply too many different kinds of unhealthy relationships for us to cover in the pages of this book. What we can do instead is learn to recognize the signs of healthy and unhealthy relationships. Based on that, we can try to change our various relationships and pursue healthier ones. Doing so will be much better for our physical health, as you've seen, but also for our mental health and overall happiness, as you're about to discover.

Chapter 2:

Benefits of Healthy

Relationships

By now, you already know that having healthy relationships is good for your health and longevity. Good social relationships have an array of other benefits to offer you, though. They're not only great for your physical health but your mental and emotional well-being, too. They tend to make you feel more connected to the world around you. They improve your sense of social connectedness, which can be defined as the sense of belonging, support, and value you get from the quality and number of the diverse types of relationships in your life (*How Does Social Connectedness Affect Health?* 2023). Good relationships and social connectedness can even be good for your community and its health. After all, a community where everyone feels like they belong will be turned into a more supportive, harmonious, and positive environment to be a part of. With this in mind, let's take an even closer look at healthy relationships and the many benefits they have to offer you, as well as the people in your life.

Mental Health Benefits

One of the key benefits healthy relationships have to offer you is that they reduce your stress and anxiety levels, as you know. One reason these relationships can do this is because the people you form relationships with offer you support when you need it, and this effectively reduces your stress levels. Another reason for this has to do with the mirror neurons in your brain. Mirror neurons are part of the reason why other people's emotions are so contagious. When you see a person displaying a certain emotion, like joy, and acting to reflect it, like smiling, the brain cells making neurons associated with that emotion and action in your brain light up. You start feeling the inklings of joy and want to smile for yourself.

There's an old saying you might have heard before: Tell me who your friends are, and I'll tell you who you are. You can see how true this saying is when you consider it in the context of mirror neurons. Say that your friends are overwhelmingly negative, pessimistic people. Putting aside the fact that you won't be able to form healthy relationships with such people, that you will start emulating their attitude and behavior is undeniable, if only because of those mirror neurons. This is why your choice of friends in life is so important. These choices will play a crucial role in how happy, stress-free, and positive you will be. Choose the right people to have in your life, and your mirror neurons will help you adopt the right behaviors (*Benefits of Social Relationships*, n.d.). Choose the wrong ones, however, and your mind will start replicating the wrong behaviors, meaning ones that will mercilessly drag you down. Healthy relationships are ones that typically lift you up rather than drag you down. That's not to say that a friend can't ever have an off day or two from time to time, but it does mean that negativity shouldn't be their default setting, at least not unless you want to suffer certain repercussions for it.

As you can gather from this, mirror neurons are powerful enough to impact your mood and, thus, play a part in your mental health. That part can be a positive or negative one depending on who your friends are, as you'll see later. These neurons, though, don't constitute the only social-neurological factor that affects your mental health and well-being. The reward centers of your brain, which make you feel good when they become activated, do as well. It's recently been proven in a study that physical touch, like a friend hugging you or patting you on the back, activates the pleasure centers of your brain (Schroeder et al., 2014). This makes you actively want to seek out social connections and form close enough relationships with them that such casual touching is the norm. Having such relationships means having your brain's reward center activated often. It also means enjoying the positive effects that this has to offer you regularly.

You may recall from the previous chapter that having low self-esteem is one of the signs that you're in a toxic relationship of some sort. Conversely, it can be said that having high levels of self-esteem is a sign that you're in a healthy relationship. Not only that, but we can go as far as to say that high self-esteem is a byproduct of healthy relationships. This claim was proven in an interesting study conducted in 2019. The study found that good social relationships helped shape a person's self-esteem over extended periods. It didn't matter if that person was 4 or 74 years old. If they had good, healthy social relationships in their lives, they were able to develop a higher sense of self-esteem (Harris, 2019). As a rule, you want to have high levels of self-esteem because it improves your emotional health and well-being, makes you more confident, makes it easier for you to make decisions, increases your motivation, and turns you into a more resilient person, ready to take on challenges (Cherry, 2021).

One of the defining characteristics of healthy relationships is that they allow you the room you need to maintain your individuality. A healthy relationship allows for ample time for yourself. That's time you can devote to practicing self-care. Practicing self-care becomes far easier to do when you have good, healthy relationships in your life. A lot of people struggle with self-care because they consider it selfish. Alternatively, they feel that they don't deserve self-care, whether they realize it or not. Good, healthy relationships do away with both these illusions. They dismantle the first one by having you show care to the people in your life. This normalizes caring behavior, effectively demonstrating it's not selfish but simply kind. They dismantle the second illusion by having you receive care from others.

Say you are in a really good, healthy romantic relationship. Your partner in this relationship will actively and willingly show you a great deal of love, consideration, and kindness. In doing so, they will make it clear, through their actions, that you are deserving of these things. This will make it possible for you to start treating yourself the same way, too. You'll start practicing self-care, whatever it may mean for you. Practicing self-care regularly will help you reduce your stress levels even more, as well as boost your energy levels and lower your odds of getting sick, to name a few of the benefits it has in store for you (Lawler, 2023).

Another core characteristic of healthy relationships is trust. Trust doesn't come automatically with a relationship. Instead, it's built slowly over time. You take a risk to trust the person with your innermost thoughts and feelings. In healthy relationships, that risk pays off. Whatever you share with the person is treated with respect. It's never taken advantage of or shared with others without your express permission. All this being the case, the trust between you and the person you've formed a relationship with increases. At the same time, your capacity to trust others increases, too. That's not to say you trust everyone you meet the moment you meet them; however, you start to see that there are trustworthy people in the world and become capable of taking a chance on them. In doing so, you get to grow your social circle and fill it with people you genuinely care about, and you form strong connections.

Social and Physical Benefits

A good relationship is a two-way street, as you know. You give as much as you take. Given that, healthy relationships require being there for others and trying to understand their thoughts, feelings, and where they're coming from. To be clear, you don't always have to agree with the people in your life. You and a good friend may have completely differing opinions on a variety of matters, and that's all right so long as you do two things: listen to one another with respect and try to understand each other's feelings and points of view. At the end of the day, you may still disagree but can do so compassionately and with empathy. As an example, say that punctuality is immensely important to a colleague of yours. They consider being punctual a sign of respect. You, however, don't worry about it that much. That's not to say you typically make people wait for you for hours on end, but you don't stress about being 5 to 10 minutes late to a meeting, particularly if it's a meeting of two. One day, you're late to a particular meeting by 10 minutes. Your colleague gets upset. You can respond in two ways in this scenario. You can dismiss what they're saying and conclude that they're making a big deal out of nothing. Or you can listen to why they're upset and explain that hurting them wasn't your intention and that you typically struggle with punctuality but promise to make more of an effort from now on.

Responding in the first way in this scenario will likely lead to a pretty big argument and may even do some damage to your working relationship. Getting into such an argument over a matter like this seems rather trivial and unnecessary. Responding in the second manner, on the other hand, will allow you and your colleague to have a genuine conversation where you come to grasp each other's perspectives. In doing so, you get to know one another a little better, work out your differences, and maybe even grow closer. At any rate, you certainly get to work better together. That's something that empathy is more than capable of achieving. Practicing and developing your empathy in this way not only helps strengthen your relationships but also increases your empathy levels in general. This is good news because being able to empathize with others translates to improving your communication skills, working better in a team, improving your leadership skills, being more compassionate to others, regardless of whether you know them or not, and more (Suttie, 2019).

The benefits we've covered so far in this chapter all have to do with your mental and emotional well-being. There are physical benefits to healthy relationships, too. One is that being in good relationships strengthens your immune system. You already know this, but did you know that healthy relationships speed up your healing process as well? This doesn't only apply to the time it takes for you to recover from an illness but also to how fast your wounds, like a cut, heal as well. At the same time, having healthy relationships lowers the amount of pain you feel as a result of that wound. Such relationships can soothe the aches and pains you feel in general, even ones that come with aging. Toxic relationships, on the other hand, do the exact opposite. They stall your healing process to the point that wounds repair themselves more slowly. They also worsen the pain they cause you. They do the same with any other pains or aches you experience in your life (Brueck, 2023).

Another fascinating benefit that comes with having a good, healthy relationship in your life has to do with sleep, of all things. Recent studies show that having healthy relationships is something that fosters quality sleep (Kent et al., 2015). It turns out that the more supportive and healthy your relationships are, the better the quality and duration of your sleep. So, if insomnia is something that plagues you regularly, then working to improve your relationship with the people in your life might help you solve this problem. The reason better relationships lead to better sleep has to do with two factors: stress and depression. Insomnia is typically a result of unresolved stress or anxiety. These two things keep your mind on high alert, even when your body is desperate for sleep. Healthy relationships, however, reduce your stress and anxiety levels, preventing them from keeping you up at night. They reduce depression, too, and do away with a lot of the isolation you might feel as a result of it. Together, all this improves your mental health considerably, making it possible for you to get a good night's rest.

There's one final social impact that good relationships have: They improve the community and environment you are living and working in. They do so by improving the individuals who are a part of that environment because you're not the only person enjoying the benefits we've covered so far. Other people do as well, which means they all get to become more positive, happy, empathetic human beings. They all get to understand one another more and communicate better than they used to. They become better able to support one another and end up creating a far more harmonious environment to exist in. By forging healthy relationships, then, you're not just doing something good for yourself. You're doing something great for the people in your life and the community you are part of.

Naturally, for this to be the case, you have to know how to forge healthy relationships with others. Knowing what a healthy relationship looks like is one thing. Being able to do it is another matter entirely, one that begins with a hard-to-execute yet very important task: setting and maintaining healthy boundaries for yourself, as you'll discover in the following chapter.

Chapter 3:

Getting to Know Your

Needs

If there's one common trait all human beings share, it's that we all want to be loved. We all want to forge close, trusting, and loving relationships with each other. Some of us are great at doing so. Others struggle with this for a variety of reasons and sometimes end up forming relationships that are less than healthy. One of the key reasons a person might do this is because they've failed to set firm boundaries going into that relationship. Odds are, they didn't set boundaries properly because they wanted to be liked. This is a common issue among new employees, for example, who want to be well-liked by their colleagues. Their desire to be liked by them causes them to put their needs on hold for theirs. This is exactly what someone who agrees to take on a colleague's workload for them, when they don't have the time to do so, is doing. At first, this isn't too big of a deal, as it's reasoned away as a one-time thing. Over time, however, it comes to define the dynamics of the relationship this person has formed. This person finds that their needs are always being put on hold and that they are bending over backward to cater to the needs and wants of their colleague, which rapidly grows to be both draining and exhausting.

Does this scenario sound familiar to you? It might be because failing to set firm boundaries with the people in our lives is a mistake many of us make. It's a common mistake because a great many people misunderstand what a boundary is. The general belief is that boundaries are a way of keeping distance from the people in our lives. According to this belief, when you establish a boundary for yourself, you prevent yourself from growing close to others. Nothing, however, could be further from the truth. Boundaries aren't tools you use to keep people at arm's length. They're tools you use to express your needs and make sure they're met. They're what you turn to when you want to ensure that your relationships are reciprocal, as all healthy relationships need to be.

The Benefits of Knowing Yourself

At its core, a boundary can be defined as a limit showing others what is acceptable and unacceptable behavior for you. It's how you show people what you need, what you're comfortable with, and how you want to be treated. It's a way for you to assert your needs and wants without getting aggressive. Boundaries, then, are a part of effective and healthy communication, just as they are a natural part of healthy relationships.

Setting boundaries for yourself is important for numerous reasons. First and foremost, they help you to stand up for your own interests, even when they don't match that of others. They help you state your needs and have them met. Without boundaries, no one will know what your needs are since you won't be communicating them. People don't have telepathic capabilities—at least not as far as we know. With boundaries, they'll be able first to understand what your needs are and then meet them.

Boundaries can also be a way of saying no to things you don't want or are unable to do. Contrary to what you may think, you don't have to say yes to every request made of you. You are allowed to say no to things, and sometimes, you must do so. Say you are very busy at work. You have a great many responsibilities you need to get through. However, if you keep on schedule, you should be able to finish everything in time and get home at a reasonable hour to rest. As you're thinking this, a colleague drops by your office. They explain that they've had an urgent matter come up, and they ask you to take some of their tasks or projects off their hands. It's an inconvenience, one that will make you stay late at the office and eat into your personal time, but you decide to be understanding and do as they ask. You get home quite late that night and practically pass out when you get to bed.

The following day, the same thing happens again. Then, again and again. Things keep going like this for quite a while. Your colleague has a valid excuse to present to you each time they knock on your door, and each time you fail to set your boundaries and fail to say no. In so doing, you consistently end up with more work than you can handle. This situation rapidly depletes you mentally and physically until, finally, you find you've completely burned out to the point that you can't do any work at all.

What would have happened if you had said no somewhere along the way? What would have happened if you'd set your boundaries on, say, the second day and said, "I helped you out once, but I can't keep doing your job for you"? Your colleague might not have loved that response, but they would have respected it. They would have had no other choice but to return to their office and do their work. Meanwhile, you would have been able to go home at a decent hour and spend your free time however you wanted, be it with friends and family, or by yourself. In either case, you would have gotten the rest you needed and deserved and would not have burned out.

Boundaries, then, help prevent conditions like burnout by giving you the ability to say no. They help you establish a good work-life balance and stave off a number of mental health conditions, ranging from burnout to chronic anxiety and depression (Koutsimani et al., 2019). This doesn't mean you can't help out a friend or a colleague once in a while when they really need it, of course. However, it does mean that you don't have to, especially if "helping out" will be detrimental to you in the end.

When you think about it, setting healthy boundaries makes it possible for you to be there for the people you care about when they need support. How? Well, imagine that you burned out because you weren't able to say no to that one colleague. Just then, a really good friend came to you in tears because they'd just broken up with their partner of over 10 years. They asked you to come over, and though part of you wanted to, you simply weren't able to muster up the energy needed to be there for them. Even if you managed to, your mind was too exhausted to properly focus on what they were saying and offer any real consolation. Alternatively, say a real emergency came up at work while you were burned out. Ordinarily, you would have been able to solve this emergency with ease. Now, however, you weren't able to do anything about it, which meant that the problem only grew to be bigger and bigger until it finally imploded.

Would either of these things have happened if you hadn't been burned out? Of course not. If you hadn't been burned out, you would have had the emotional, mental, and physical energy needed to support your friend in their time of need (Brant, 2023). You, likewise, would have had the energy you needed to roll up your sleeves at work and get to work solving whatever crisis it was you were facing. Setting boundaries, then, doesn't only help you. It helps the people around you by allowing you to conserve your energy and use it when they need your time, support, and effort. Setting boundaries makes you a better friend, colleague, and team member overall.

Your boundaries protect you in a variety of different ways, as you might have gathered. The burnout example demonstrates how they protect your mental and physical health. Boundaries protect your emotional health, too. They do so by having you draw a line that shows others how they are to talk to you and act toward you. This achieves two things. First, it allows you to identify those individuals who are willing to respect your emotional boundaries. Those are the individuals you want in your life and you can get close to. They're the ones you'll form healthy relationships with. Second, it reinforces the message that your emotions and emotional needs are just as important as those of others. It helps you to recognize those needs and take measures to meet them yourself through acts of self-care. Setting boundaries ends up increasing your self-compassion, self-esteem, and self-confidence.

Setting healthy boundaries is good for your relationships, too, in that it keeps them from growing toxic. It does this by allowing you the time you need to retain your individuality. You can use that time and space to pursue your own interests, engage in self-care, and spend time with other loved ones. This prevents your relationship from becoming codependent. At the same, by having you state your needs and wants, boundaries establish your identity for others to see. This allows others to understand you better, respond to your needs the same way you respond to theirs, and grasp what behaviors you aren't comfortable with. All this enhances the communication between you and others. At the same time, it allows you to see that other people do respect your boundaries. This inevitably increases your trust in others, as well as your conviction that you and your needs matter. For all these reasons, setting boundaries often improves relationships rather than hinders or weakens them.

Learning What You Need

All of this is contingent on your ability to set boundaries, of course. To set good personal boundaries for yourself, you need to first figure out what your needs are. To that end, you have to reflect on why you want to set boundaries in the first place. Why are boundaries important to you? Why do you feel the need to set them now? How do you want the boundaries you set to help you emotionally, mentally, and even physically? Consider these questions carefully. If you want, try journaling about them or at least writing down the answers you come up with. If writing is not your thing, you can try meditating on it, too. The key here is to think carefully about your answer so you can identify your needs (Pattemore, 2021).

Asking these questions is one way of figuring out what your needs are so you can set your boundaries. There are others. One is to make a comprehensive list of all your personal values. Healthy boundaries will always be based on your values. If they're not, then they probably never were *your* boundaries. Rather, they had been imposed on you at some point. So, by listing and defining your values, you can identify the very starting point of your needs and boundaries. You can then start shaping and, later, expressing them.

Another way to determine your needs is to look at your past relationships. What worked in those relationships? What didn't? In which instances did you feel most seen, heard, respected, and cared for in those relationships? In which relationships did you least feel such things? In answering these questions, you can see which of your needs were met and which ones weren't. You can then use that information to navigate your way as you formulate your boundaries. You can similarly reflect on what makes you feel most loved and respected in your current relationships. This will unveil your needs for you to see, just as interrogations of your past relationships will.

The same can be said for reflecting on moments when you feel really happy, sad, or even angry. Anger may seem like negative emotions, but it's a very useful tool. A person usually feels most angry when a need of theirs isn't met, making them feel as though they're being disregarded. Anger is a key indicator to pay heed to in this case. So, when was the last time you felt really angry? Where did that anger come from? If it was when someone was 30 minutes late to a dinner party and didn't let you know, then odds are they crossed a boundary in that instance. Perhaps their lateness and refusal to inform you on time was a sign of disrespect for you. Perhaps it made you feel like you were an afterthought. Perhaps what you need, then, is for the people in your life to show that you are important to them by being on time or letting you know in advance if and when they're going to be late.

A last measure you can take to discover your needs is to consider different situations you've been in where you ended with saying, "I wish I'd said no to this." What made you uncomfortable in that situation? What did that situation cost you? How would you have preferred that situation to go, or how would you have wanted to spend your time if you hadn't been stuck in that situation? By reflecting on such questions, you can identify instances where you failed to set a boundary. You can then get to figuring out what boundary could have helped you in that scenario. Having done that, you can move on to the real task, which is to start establishing your boundaries.

Setting boundaries can be a scary undertaking, especially if you're not used to it. You might want to start with a few relatively small boundaries, as that will be less daunting. Once you set them, you can observe that they actually do work and are well received. This will boost your confidence a bit, allowing you to build on the boundaries you've already set and increase them however you want, bit by bit. You must take this process slowly to get used to setting boundaries, reflect on their results properly, and make any adjustments you deem necessary as you keep going.

The key thing to remember about boundaries is that you need to be consistent with them if they are to work. If you set a boundary one day and only uphold it sometimes, then your behavior will give rise to a lot of confusion around you. People will be confused about whether something they're doing or saying is making you uncomfortable or not. In other words, they won't be able to understand if they're crossing a boundary. How could they when you treat the boundaries you set as if they were jump ropes? If you want to prevent such confusion and make sure your boundaries are always respected, then you have to be consistent. You have to communicate them clearly, firmly tell people when they're crossing a boundary, and take whatever protective action is necessary then and there.

As an extension of that, you have to tell people when they are crossing a boundary you've set. It may be that the person didn't know something was a boundary for you. It may be that they forgot somehow. It may also be that they are willfully crossing your boundary. In the first case scenario, you don't have to get too mad. All you have to do is tell someone that they're crossing a boundary and warn them. After all, everyone's boundaries are different, and it's perfectly possible that someone would cross yours without realizing it. In the second case, you have to remind people of your boundaries firmly but not too harshly. People sometimes forget things, especially if it's new information or under hectic conditions. So, assuming someone has crossed a boundary because they forgot or by mistake, simply talking to them about it should suffice to fix the situation, so long as that person doesn't get into the habit of repeating the same mistake over and over.

What if the person is willingly and consciously crossing your boundaries, though? This is the one scenario where you have to be very firm and clear. If someone is ignoring your boundaries and crossing them intentionally, that's a clear sign that they don't respect them. It's also a clear sign that they will do so again. Now, this is not necessarily something people do out of malice. Some people might hear a boundary and decide it's "stupid" simply because it's not a boundary they have. Such people tend to have low levels of empathy and find it hard to understand that crossing a boundary you set is hurtful to you. While you don't necessarily have to cut such people from your life, the clear disrespect they show for your boundaries is reason enough to distance yourself from them. Crossing someone's boundaries means ignoring their needs and wants, maliciously or not. That can be very hurtful, and it's not something you should be subjected to. It's understandable and even necessary that you pull away from such people and, if need be, go as far as to cut them out of your life.

That, however, is an extreme measure you typically won't have to resort to. Most people will understand and respect your boundaries so long as you communicate them clearly. One thing that may help people to grasp your boundaries and what they're about is to set them early on. Doing so will set the norm and tone for relationships. Of course, if you're new to setting boundaries, this won't be something you'll get to do with your pre-existing relationships. It will be a policy you can adopt for any new ones moving forward.

One thing to remember about boundaries is that they vary from person to person. That means two things. First, it means that the boundaries you set for yourself may be very different from the ones that others set for themselves. Second, it means that the boundaries you set for your colleagues will be different from the ones you set for your friends, siblings, family, partner, and so on. This is because you have different relationships with all these people, and you enjoy different levels of closeness with them. It's understandable that the boundaries you set for, say, your boss wouldn't be the same as the ones you set for your romantic partner of

12 years. This being the case, you should always consider whom you're dealing with when setting a boundary. If you're comfortable with where a boundary is with someone, then it can remain where it is. If you feel that you are closer to them than others, though, you can set a different boundary for them, so long as you are comfortable with that.

Another thing to remember about boundaries is that they can change over time. Say you made a new friend. You enjoy their company, and they seem trustworthy enough. You're not very close with them, though, since you don't know them very well yet. Then, as time goes by, you grow closer and closer with them. You learn a great deal about them, and they share a lot of very personal things with you, showing you that they trust you. You reciprocate that trust. After a while, you realize that you've become really good friends with them. So, you adjust the boundaries you have because your boundaries for new acquaintances are different from the ones for close friends.

As an example, the amount of time you spend talking to an acquaintance is not the same as the amount of time you spend talking to a close friend. Similarly, the depth of the conversation you enjoy with a close friend is very different than the one you enjoy with an acquaintance. If the friend in this example had suddenly asked you, on day one of your meeting, how your marriage was going, you likely would not have answered that question, thinking it was too personal. Put another way, you would have considered the question a breach of your boundaries. If they asked you this question after you'd become close friends, though, you might have opened up to them and shared your marital troubles with them. You wouldn't have considered the question a breach of boundaries because the boundaries between the two of you would have changed by then.

Now, as for what type of boundaries you want to set, this depends on you and what you're comfortable with. What one person is willing to share with their closest friends is very different from what another is willing to share with them. As a rule, you neither want to be too rigid with your boundaries, to the point that you don't share anything with others, or too lax, to the point that you overshare. What you want to do is share only as much as you're comfortable with. Your comfort is your most important guide and measuring stick where boundaries are concerned. If you feel uncomfortable sharing something with someone or saying yes to a request they've made of you, that's a clear sign your boundaries are being stepped over and you should take a step back.

Now that you know the basics of setting boundaries, let's take a closer look at its nuances. Boundaries are quite complicated, as you've seen, if for no other reason than they're very personal. Setting your boundaries starts with determining your needs. You then need to translate those needs into boundaries, which is where the real work begins, as you'll soon see.

Chapter 4:

Setting Personal

Boundaries

Setting boundaries with the people in your life, particularly ones you care about, can be rather challenging. This is partly because of the misconception that boundaries mean distancing yourself from others, as mentioned before. This isn't the only misconception surrounding boundaries, though. There are others, like fear of missing out (FOMO), for instance (Lee, 2018). FOMO is a legitimate psychological condition where you fear you'll be missing out on a valuable opportunity or a really fun time by saying no to someone. Sometimes FOMO can prove helpful to you in that it pushes you to say yes to an offer that proves very worthwhile. This is not the case for those times when you have other responsibilities, like an important project you have to finish at work, that you need to tend to first. It's also not the case when you're too drained to participate in whatever it is you're saying yes to.

FOMO is a genuine fear, one that can make you disregard your boundaries if you let it. It's just as dangerous as perfectionism, which can similarly make you disregard your boundaries or even prevent you from setting them in the first place. People who are perfectionists have a fear of letting people down. They despise the feeling because it implies that they are less than perfect. To avoid this feeling, they refrain from setting boundaries and saying no to others, even when they need to. They consider saying no a sign of weakness, proving that they're not strong enough to do it all. As a result, they put themselves under an immense amount of pressure. That pressure never really goes away, at least not until one of two things happens: You either learn to set boundaries and say no, or you burn out completely.

A final reason why people struggle to set boundaries has to do with social conditioning. We live in a world where our sense of identity is all too often tied to what we're able to do for others. This goes double for women, who are expected by society to be "caring" and "giving" and who are judged or penalized in various ways when they're not. When we consider the society we live in, it's easy to see how it might make it difficult for people to put themselves first and set boundaries. It's equally as easy to see how saying no to something or someone can make a person feel incredibly guilty, even when the thing they're saying no to is pretty insignificant in retrospect.

How to Set Boundaries and Not Feel Guilty

So, how do we overcome these obstacles? How do we make it so we can set healthy boundaries for ourselves without being afraid, feeling like a failure, or feeling guilty? Achieving this is a bit of a process. All processes, though, begin with a first step, and your first step here is to discover what needs you are trying to meet in setting your boundaries. That's what you learned how to do in the previous chapter.

There are some additional steps you can take to gain better clarity of your needs if you'd like. For instance, you can start thinking a little more carefully about your emotions and the various things that trigger them. Remember how anger was a guidepost for unmet needs? Truthfully, anger isn't the only emotion that's linked to your needs. Fear is, too. Consider FOMO. When you experience FOMO, what you're experiencing isn't missing out on a fun time; it's missing out on the opportunity to fulfill one of your needs. If that's the case, then thinking carefully about what need you're trying to fulfill by saying yes to something should help you.

Say it's a networking event you have FOMO about. Is it possible that what you really need is some social interaction and rest since you've been working so hard? Is it possible what you need is to feel connected to others, particularly those you haven't seen in a long time who will be at that event? Alternatively, is it possible that you are afraid of missing out on the opportunity to bond with some really good contacts there? Assuming these are the case, these are easy needs to meet. You can review your schedule to see what responsibilities you can take off your plate to give yourself more free time to rest and socialize. You can reach out to the people you want to see and tell them you won't be able to be at the event but you'd really like to see them. Similarly, you can reach out to the people you want to network with and schedule some one-on-one time with them, which will be more effective in the long run for you. You can then arrange a separate time to meet after you're done with your work.

Other emotions can help you to figure out your needs, too. Happiness and joy are emotions you feel when your needs are met. Thinking back on instances when you experienced these emotions and what triggered them should help you greatly. Meanwhile, thinking back on moments when you felt disappointed and sad should come in handy, too, since it's not always going to be the anger you feel when your needs are unmet. Thinking about moments when you feel drained, on the other hand, should show you when you're failing to say no to things you don't enjoy or have time for. Commitments that you truly don't want to participate in can be incredibly draining, more so than any other event. You have to make a mental and emotional effort to pretend to want to be there, after all. Not only that, but you have to constantly grapple with negative emotions such as irritation and perhaps even guilt for wanting to leave.

These feelings can take an additional toll, leaving you completely exhausted by the time you're done.

All these markers can be used to identify your needs. With that out of the way, the time will have finally come to set boundaries that will ensure those needs are met. By now, you know you can use your values to do this, but what exactly does that look like, and how does it work? Well, your boundaries are the rules you live by. You use those rules to decide how you act and behave, as well as how others are allowed to act toward and talk to you. These rules must be based on your values for them to apply to you. Lucky for you, you've already listed and defined your values. Now, you can prioritize them.

Let's assume you wrote down 20 values. Which of the items you've listed are the most important to you? Try to narrow that list down to your top 10 and then the top 5. If you can, narrow things down even further to your top 3. Once you've done so, the ones you will be left with will be your core values. These are the guiding stars of your life. They are the guiding stars of your boundaries, too, at least so long as you ask yourself, "Does this boundary align with my core values?" as you're setting them. You don't only use your values when you're setting boundaries, though. You can also ask yourself whether something someone is asking you to do falls in line with your core values. If the answer to that question is no, then you can freely say no to whatever request has been made of you.

This is, admittedly, a very introspective approach to discovering your needs and setting your boundaries. Funnily enough, there is another, more extroverted method you can use to do this, and that's to use the people in your life as reference points. You can't just use anyone in your life for this. You can only use those individuals you respect. Consider the people you respect carefully for a minute. Odds are, they emulate the very values you hold dear. That's why you respect them so much. If your boundaries are based on your values, and if the people you respect have the same values as you, that means you can consider their behaviors as guideposts in and of themselves. You can start imitating and adopting those same behaviors. In doing so, you'll get to act according to your values. You'll be able to observe what these people's boundaries look like and start adopting them yourself.

Looking to others when trying to set boundaries can be a very useful trick. Still, the best resource to turn to in personal matters such as this is always yourself. More accurately, it's your past experiences. Remember how you could look to past experiences to identify when you felt most drained? You can similarly look to times when you felt over-exhausted or overextended. You can then question those instances to discover what happened that made you feel like that. Often, you'll find that you said yes to too many things and depleted all your energy as a result. So, what could you have said no to? In which moments could you have put your needs before other people's wants? Identifying such moments is important because it helps prepare you for similar instances in the future. It provides you with a solid reason why you should say no to similar requests, should they ever be made, and what the consequences will be if you refrain from doing so. In other words, it helps you identify not only boundaries you can set but also the right opportunities where you can implement them.

Conversely, you can also think about instances that give, rather than deplete, your energy. When do you feel most energetic and enthusiastic to work or do something? When do you feel most ambitious or driven? By asking yourself these questions, you discover how your behavior and attitude change when your needs are met. You get to see how much more productive and how much happier you become when this happens, which gives you an added incentive to start drawing boundaries. These positive effects you observe help you counter any guilt you might feel at the thought of drawing boundaries and help break down your resistance toward them.

A similar logic can be applied to the people in your life. We all have two kinds of people who enter our lives: those who respect our boundaries and those who don't. These two types of individuals affect us in very different ways. People who respect our boundaries make us feel safe and secure. They make us feel both trusted and supported. Being with them makes us happy. We feel energized when we're with them. We enjoy spending time with them and are comfortable by their side. That's not what happens with people who don't respect our boundaries. If anything, we feel the exact opposite way where these people are concerned. This is important to make note of because that feeling of discomfort is what we can use to identify such people. Once we do, we'll have a choice to make: Do we want to distance ourselves from these people or cut them out of our lives entirely? Making such a decision might be hard, but, truthfully, remaining close to people who like testing and crossing our boundaries is even harder. Such people are draining, to say the least, and choosing to spend time with them equals agreeing to feel drained all the time. So, why should you subject yourself to such treatment?

The methods we have covered so far are great for identifying your boundaries. Once you have identified them, you will have to communicate them to others. Otherwise, people won't know what your boundaries are. They will, therefore, be likely to cross them without realizing it since everyone's boundaries are different. Communicating your needs and boundaries is essential for your ability to create and maintain healthy relationships; but it can be a little tricky, especially if you're nervous about it. The key thing to remember when communicating your boundaries and needs is that you have to be as clear as you can be about them.

Say you live with your mom. She's lovely, but she has a habit of treating you like you are a kid rather than a grown adult. As such, she has a habit of barging into your room without knocking. She has caught you in the middle of important work meetings, while working out, and even in flagrante delicto on more than one occasion. This bothers you, and you feel the need to set a boundary. So, you sit your mother down and tell her that you need some personal space. You may think that this communicates your message clearly, but it doesn't. This is because your mother can interpret this in several ways. She can take it to mean you don't want to spend as much time with her and, therefore, start spending more time with her friends. Given her misinterpretation, she will likely continue walking into your room whenever she feels like it.

How could you express your boundary and the main need it stems from in a way that makes it clear? One way to do this might be, "I feel uncomfortable and disrespected when you barge into my room without even knocking. I would appreciate it if you would knock and wait for me to say, 'Come in' before entering my room from now on" (Reid, 2023). As you can see, unlike the "personal space" statement, this explanation leaves no room for misinterpretation. It makes your needs crystal clear. It establishes why this is an important need for you and sets very clear expectations of behavior moving forward. Those expectations can then be met and your boundaries can be respected.

One thing you may have noticed about the example statement we've used here is that it starts with "I feel." There's such a thing as "I feel" statements. These are ways of expressing your unmet needs that effectively communicate how a certain type of behavior makes you feel without seeming to blame or accuse the person before you. Generally, you want to use "I feel" statements when explaining your boundaries because it turns the focus on you. Since such statements refrain from assigning blame to others, they keep them from becoming defensive. They make them more likely to listen to you and truly hear and understand what you have to say. They make them likely to adjust their behavior so your boundaries aren't crossed and your needs are met moving forward.

As you can see from all this, the way you express your boundaries is just as important as expressing them.

Your delivery can play a major part in how your words are received. When you choose to communicate, your boundaries can play a critical role in this, too. Expressing your boundaries in the middle of a heated fight, for instance, is probably not a good idea, as your words either won't be properly heard or they'll be misconstrued as an attack, even if you are using "I feel" statements. What you want to do, then, is choose the right moment to communicate your boundaries. The right moment to do this is a calm one, when both you and your conversation partner feel relaxed and are in the kind of headspace where you can hear each other out. Arranging to discuss boundaries in such a moment is always a good idea. If you find that things are growing heated, you can always press pause and back away a bit. In doing so, you can give one another the physical space you need to calm down. Once the both of you have calmed down, you can revisit the conversation with cooler heads.

There's one last thing you'll need to do when communicating your boundaries if you want to ensure that they are respected, and that's to answer any questions your conversation partner might have. While you may be making an effort to be as clear as possible, there may be certain things your conversation partner hasn't grasped or is confused about. Taking the time you need to answer these questions will help to dispel confusion and prevent any accidental boundary crossings as a result. Likewise, you can ask your conversation partner follow-up questions to check in and see how they feel about what you've discussed and make sure they understood what you were trying to communicate.

How to Maintain Your Boundaries

Setting your boundaries is one thing. Maintaining them is another. Maintaining boundaries can be just as tough as setting them because it requires consistency, as you know. You can't enforce a boundary one day, completely forget about it the next, and expect it to be respected the day after. You have to be both clear and firm about your boundaries, as well as vocal when they are willingly or unwittingly crossed. To that end, you have to be clear about what the consequences of crossing your boundaries are.

Say you have a colleague who has a rather foul mouth. They curse a lot, and often, they curse the person they're talking to. They don't mean anything bad by it, but they cuss out their conversation partners regardless. Some people would be all right with this. You are not. You are bothered by the fact that your work friend cusses at you as they talk to you and find their demeanor to be very unprofessional and unbecoming of a workplace. So, you tell them as much, and you ask them to stop. They are confused by this and tell you they can't stop. "This is just how I am. It's how I talk to everyone," they tell you. That does not change the fact that you are uncomfortable with this behavior and that this is a boundary for you. If your work friend insists on talking to you this way, then that will mean they'll be knowingly crossing the boundary they've been given. That is something that must have consequences, at least if this is a real boundary for you.

A real-life consequence of your work friend talking to you in a manner that you dislike would be them not getting to talk to you as much anymore. In other words, it means fewer coffee and lunch breaks with them or hallway chats. If they are going to insist on treating you in a way that upsets you, why should you spend time with them and become upset in the process? Of course, you can't simply cut your work friend out of your life in this case. They still exist in the same work environment as you, after all. Instead, you have to tell them you will limit your contact with them and cut off contact, as much as it's possible at the office, if they persist with this type of treatment. You have to make it clear that this will be the consequence of their choice to ignore a boundary you've clearly explained to them. They will now have a choice to make: Either they will remedy their behavior, or they will accept this consequence and lose your friendship as a result.

To be clear, not all consequences have to be this harsh. Different boundary violations may come with different consequences. One consequence may be not spending as much time with someone as you used to. Another might be refraining from telling them personal matters, which might be a consequence of someone violating your privacy or breaking your trust. Whatever the consequence of crossing a specific boundary is, you must be clear and firm about them. That's not to say you can't be compassionate when dealing with such situations. Sometimes, people make an honest mistake and unintentionally cross a boundary. To go back to the "living with your mother" example, your mother will likely make an honest effort to respect your new boundary. However, having grown used to barging into your room willy-nilly, it'll take her a while to get used to these new habits. Along the way, she'll probably slip up a couple of times. Blowing a gasket or threatening to move out at the first infraction won't help you. Firmly but compassionately reminding her of her mistake will. If it does not, and her behavior remains unchanged, then it might be time to consider serious consequences, ranging from locking your door to actually moving out. There is a difference between being compassionate and being a pushover, after all.

Setting and maintaining boundaries has a lot to do with clear communication, as you've seen. Communication is a hard art to master. Yet, it's one that we must master and not just for the sake of our boundaries. Clear, healthy communication is a vital part of any relationship. Master this art form and you will be surprised at how many healthy, supportive relationships you can develop. What exactly goes into healthy communication, and what are its benefits anyway? This subject merits its own chapter, which is why we should now turn the page.

Chapter 5:

Communicating Effectively

Have you ever felt as though you were talking to a wall or the wind? Has there ever been a time when you felt like your words weren't being heard at all? If so, you've experienced some of the damaging effects poor communication can have on you and your relationships. Poor communication is the bane of any relationship. It's sure to ensure that your relationship either crumbles to dust over time or completely and spontaneously implodes in an instant. As always, this applies to every type of relationship, from friendships and romantic partnerships to business relationships and family dynamics. When taken in this context, it's easy to see that poor communication can impact your life and social well-being in pretty significant ways. It can, for instance, cause you to have a falling out with a good friend. It can lead to massive arguments that disrupt the peace in your family home. It can cost you business deals and valuable opportunities. Poor communication with strangers can result in you getting into unnecessary and overheated arguments that spoil your mood for the rest of the day or even end with you getting hurt.

If poor communication is capable of doing all this, then good, effective communication should be capable of achieving the exact opposite. What does effective communication look like, though? What are its defining characteristics, and how does it work? What, specifically, are its benefits, and how can it help you in both the short and the long term? In other words, why should you care?

Why Does Communication Matter?

Good, healthy relationships are built on trust and allow you to keep building trust. There are a couple of ways you can build trust in a relationship, but the most powerful and effective of them all is communication. When done right, communication helps you foster the trust of others. This is because it allows you to use your listening skills to truly understand others and their unique perspectives, even when you don't necessarily agree with them. It allows you to use these listening skills to show people that you respect them and their opinions. This gives you access to more diverse information when making decisions, allowing you to take other people's interests and pain points into account.

Another reason why communication builds trust is that it helps you understand and respect other people's boundaries, just as it helps others to do the same with yours. This counts as another benefit of effective communication, too, and it's part of the reason why effective communication strengthens your relationships. The other reason for this is that it enables you to truly understand the people you're forming relationships with and vice versa (Smith, 2021). Closeness comes from openness and honesty, as we've already seen. Openness and honesty can only be conveyed through communication. So, master communication, and you will undeniably be able to forge stronger connections with people.

This won't just be good for your friendship and the like but for your work life, too. Building stronger, more trusting relationships with your colleagues means being able to collaborate better with them. Good communication is something that can make you a better team player, as well as a better leader if you happen to be in a leadership position. Effective communication can do this for no other reason than because it reduces any misunderstandings and disagreements you and your colleagues may have. Misunderstanding often arises when essential information isn't relayed clearly and understandably. Mistakes are made as a result, and various things get left undone, putting everyone in a tight spot because it was not initially understood that they should be done. Proper communication nips this problem in the bud, thereby reducing mistakes and preventing the arguments they can lead to.

A very interesting side effect of good communication is that it increases your level of self-awareness. It enables you to understand other people's perceptions of you. It helps you see how your words and actions affect others. This, in turn, empowers you to re-evaluate your behavior objectively and remedy it where necessary. Good communication increases your level of empathy and only accentuates this effect. Good communication is just as much about listening to others as it is about talking. When you consciously and actively listen to others—which you have to do if you want to practice healthy communication—you grasp their feelings, thoughts, circumstances, and mindsets better. You become able to put yourself in their shoes, which is what empathy is all about. You become able to alter and adjust your behavior in light of what you've discovered and, in leadership positions, make decisions that consider everyone's circumstances and benefits, as opposed to that of a single person or group.

All of this doesn't in any way mean that good communication can help you avoid arguments because doing so is impossible, at least in a healthy relationship (BetterHelp Editorial Team, 2023). That might sound contradictory to some, but the mark of a healthy relationship isn't a lack of arguments it's how arguments are handled. People usually fear arguments because they can be catastrophic when handled poorly. Things can be said in the heat of the moment that can prove very hurtful, so much so that they can damage and rupture relationships.

When handled properly, however, conflict and arguments can be a way of addressing important problems. For this to be possible, proper communication is key, as it can help de-escalate the situation, preventing you from saying hurtful things you don't mean. Good communication can allow you and the person you were arguing with to hit pause, take a moment to cool off, and calmly express the reason for your discontent without seeming to attack. Ultimately, good communication can make it possible to get to the root of a conflict and solve it before things get out of hand and feelings are hurt.

Considering the things that good communication is capable of, it's easy to see why it would bring people together and increase their overall satisfaction levels. Good communication builds trust, for instance, and it also increases your positivity. This improves both your day-to-day and long-term mood and morale, thereby contributing to your happiness, satisfaction, and wellness levels. All this increases your motivation, too, especially at work, and makes you more productive. This is precisely why workplaces value good communication and harmonious work environments so much. They recognize that good communication both reduces people's tendency to make mistakes and that happy people make for motivated employees who can do better work. They additionally recognize that effective communication skills boost people's innovation and creativity levels.

The link between creativity and communication might be a little difficult to see at first, but it is there. When you have good communication skills, you become able to convey new, valuable ideas to people (Mehndiratta Kappal, 2020). Your colleagues around you begin to do the same. They then gain the ability to take those ideas you've shared with them and use them in innovative, unexpected ways that will help them solve an existing problem or come up with another new idea. You gain the same ability. By listening to your colleagues, you obtain new information, insights, and perspectives.

How to Become a Better Communicator

Good communication is an important part of your work, social, and home life, but what does being a good communicator mean? How can you become a better communicator? You can start by thinking carefully about what you want to convey in a conversation, discussion, or even argument. Now, granted, you're not going to have the opportunity to carefully think about and outline everything you want to say before every single conversation you're going to have. However, you can certainly do so before important conversations. If you're going to have a discussion on boundaries and what yours are with someone, for instance, then you're going to want to reflect on your needs. You're also going to want to think about how you can frame your needs, using "I feel" statements in a way that you're understood but don't appear to be attacking the other person.

Conversations, particularly delicate or important ones, tend to go better when you think carefully about what you want to say and how you want to say it. You can write down bullet points of what you want to convey before really important discussions and use them as a guide through your conversation. As you're working on these bullet points or simply thinking about how to structure a conversation, you want to spare some time to determine what your objectives are. What do you want to achieve by having this conversation? Are you trying to resolve a misunderstanding? Are you trying to establish a boundary? Are you trying to understand a mistake you made at work so you don't repeat it and can make up for it? Are you working on a project with someone and trying to make sure everyone understands their tasks and assignments clearly so there are no misunderstandings or mistakes? Are you trying to do something else entirely?

Whatever the case, considering your objectives before diving into a conversation will help you keep the conversation focused. It'll keep you and your conversation partner from getting sidetracked, saving you both a lot of time and energy. Most importantly, it'll guarantee that you address every important point you want to address and resolve any problems you want to resolve.

It's important that you share everything you want to share in a conversation instead of bottling things in. However, it's just as important that you listen to whatever your conversation partner has to say. Otherwise, you'll get stuck in a very one-sided conversation. If you've been on the opposite side of such a conversation, where you couldn't even get a word in edgewise, you know how frustrating that can be. You also know how this kind of dynamic can make you feel like what you have to say is unimportant or that the person before you doesn't care about you enough to listen. That's not something you ever want someone you care about and have formed some type of relationship with to feel when speaking with you.

Not listening to others when you're speaking to them often conveys the message that you don't care or respect what they want to say. Listening to them, on the other hand, does the opposite. Not only that, but it also has certain advantages to offer you. If you're in an argument or debate, for instance, it gives you the ability to produce effective counterarguments once you're done listening (Wool, 2021). It reduces your chances of saying things you'll regret or things that might come across as insensitive later on, which can be a hairy issue to deal with at work. It gives you greater insight and information than you had before, which you can use in a myriad of ways later on. In small talk or simple conversation scenarios at networking events, it allows you to ask open-ended questions based on what you're being told and keep the conversation going rather than succumb to the dreaded awkward silence.

It must be said here that there's a difference between listening and active listening. If you're only paying attention to half of what's being said and your attention is wandering off elsewhere in the meantime, then you're not listening; you're only pretending to. The same goes for when you're thinking about what responses you're going to give to someone while they're still talking. These are easy pitfalls to fall into, but there is a way to avoid them. It's to be fully present in the moment and conversation by practicing active listening, a technique you'll find out about, at length, in the next chapter.

A conversation is a two-way street. Both parties have to listen to one another and speak in equal measure to maintain a healthy dialogue. There are certain things, however, that can derail a conversation and either cause it to implode or ground it to a halt. The most obvious example of this is openly insulting someone mid-conversation, thereby bringing a perfectly civil exchange to a sudden halt. Not all conversation derailers, though, are quite so obvious. Some are a little more subtle. Your attitude when speaking would number among those more subtle factors that have the potential to derail a conversation.

Your attitude is the way you speak to someone, and it can drastically change the meaning of your words. Consider the words "I can't believe you did that." Depending on your attitude, you can convey a variety of different meanings through those words. You can convey that you're genuinely surprised. You can convey the exact opposite of that by being sarcastic. You can imply shock, anger, or joy, depending on your tone of voice. This is important to bear in mind because the attitude you opt for when speaking to someone can either make them eager to keep the conversation going or to end it immediately. Should someone sense you're angry, they'll be pretty eager to walk away, for instance.

If there's one attitude that has the power to end conversations quickly, it's lecturing. As a rule, unless you're delivering an actual lecture in an auditorium, you do not want to come across as if you're lecturing people. Similarly, you want to make people feel and realize that you're talking *with* them, not *at* them. Talking *to* someone results in a dynamic where people are continually reacting to things you're telling them. They do not get to share anything with you of their own volition. Meanwhile, talking *with* people has both you and your conversation partner sharing and reacting in equal measure. It achieves a kind of balance, where even if everyone doesn't spend the same time talking, everyone feels they've shared everything they wanted to say. Nobody feels left out, ignored, talked down to, or like they have nothing significant to contribute. Everyone leaves the conversation feeling content.

A key sign that you're lecturing people, perhaps without meaning to, is that they're responding to you with a lot of "uh huh," "sure," and the like. Finding yourself in this kind of dynamic is a sure sign you're monopolizing the conversation and probably boring people. If nothing else, you're probably not allowing them to contribute anything of their own (McKay, 2018). A quick way to fix this is to take a pause or several as you talk to allow them to share their thoughts or opinions. Another would be to ask for them. Remember, if you are the only person speaking in a conversation in any meaningful way, then that's not a conversation; it's a lecture, speech, or sermon, in which case you should be on a pulpit.

Since the way you communicate with people is just as important as what you communicate to them, your tone of voice is something to bear in mind, too. Speaking in an aggressive tone of voice, for example, is sure to drive people away from you. It gives the sense that you are angry at them, even if you aren't, prompting them to keep their distance rather than engage in conversation. If you want to come across as approachable and easy to talk to—especially with those you've never had a conversation with before and who don't know you—then you want to maintain a neutral, friendly tone of voice as you talk. That's not to say your emotions, like excitement, shouldn't be reflected in your voice when you feel them. It just means that a neutral tone should color your voice for the most part.

Maintaining a neutral tone of voice is a communication strategy that can help you get the information you want across very clearly and in a balanced manner. Far from being robotic or monotone, it comes across as a positive, inviting, and friendly tone, which makes conversations go more smoothly. It proves effective in different conversation settings, too, like work environments, when you're meeting new people at social gatherings, or when you're chatting with a group of people. It's the preferred tone of voice for most scenarios, especially work settings, because it reduces the chance that there'll be misunderstandings in a conversation. If you're wondering what a neutral voice sounds like, it's typically one that's devoid of bias and emotional inflections—again, without sounding robotic. People speaking in a neutral tone maintain an even pitch and volume. They stick to objective words and phrasings and try to communicate information in as clear and concise a manner as possible (Durant, 2023).

Speaking in a neutral tone of voice does not mean you're not being transparent. Transparency is a vital part of being open and honest and, therefore healthy communication. Transparent communication requires being open about both positive and negative information. Owning up to a mistake you made is a good example of transparent communication. Sincerely expressing your gratitude to someone for helping you to fix that mistake is another. A great many people find transparency to be difficult. They think that doing things like owning up to your mistakes conveys weakness and lessens the trust people place in you. Yet, this is not the case. If anything, owning up to your mistakes when you make them is liable to increase people's trust in you because it demonstrates that you hold yourself accountable for your actions.

This is one of the reasons why transparent communication increases trust among people, a decided benefit of the practice. Other benefits are that transparent communication makes people better team players, encourages conversation partners to be equally as transparent, increases the sharing of ideas, and increases creativity and innovation (Hutchinson, 2020).

Transparent communication works best when you make an effort in conversation to relate to other people's feelings and make the conversation about them when you can. In other words, this communication type functions best when you're not only talking about yourself but also taking an interest in others. You already know you shouldn't monopolize a conversation—at least not if you want to keep it going. What you may not know is how you can keep from doing that. The trick here is something known as open-ended questions, which we briefly mentioned before. Open-ended questions are inquiries that don't have a specific, pre-determined answer that can keep a conversation going and deepen it. The question "Are you hungry? It is not an open-ended question, for instance, but a closed one. There are only two replies you can give: yes or no. "What did you do this weekend?" however, it is an open-ended question because there's a whole host of answers you can give, none of which your conversation partner can guess in advance. What's more, the answer you give can be used to ask even more open-ended questions. So, if you were to reply with "I went to the movies," your conversation partner can ask you things like, "What movie did you see?" "Did you enjoy it?" and "Who did you go with?"

When you're talking to someone, you want to try asking open-ended questions as much as possible. This goes double for anyone you've only just met and don't know a thing about. Open-ended questions keep conversations from becoming boring. They prevent you from falling into the dreaded awkward silence and allow you to take an actual interest in the person you're talking to. In the process, it helps you get to know them better and use empathy where appropriate (Cooks-Campbell, 2022). Empathy is your ability to understand how other people think and feel, and it's a skill you want to use in communication. It increases how well you understand someone and allows you to grow closer to them.

The thing is, though, not everyone knows how to convey empathy mid-conversation. You don't want to appear to cut someone off while they're talking, after all. Similarly, understanding where someone is coming from can be challenging since you have never lived through their circumstances. Luckily, there are a couple of things you can do to overcome both of these hurdles. To communicate your empathy without interrupting your conversation partner, you have to rely on your body language. Maintaining eye contact as someone is talking to you, slightly leaning toward them as they do so, and keeping an open posture with your arms uncrossed and your body relaxed gives the message that you're interested in, paying attention to, and invested in what's being said. It relays the message that you're fully present and there for the person who is speaking to you, all without you having to say a single word.

What if you're having trouble relating to what someone is telling you? In such cases, you will have to use your words to seek greater understanding. Specifically, you will have to ask questions like "Do I have it right that you...?" or "Can you help me understand why you feel like...?" (Yi Wong, 2021). By asking targeted questions like these, you can both confirm that you're understanding your conversation partner correctly and ensure you grasp the triggers and reasons behind their emotions. You can become more empathetic while growing closer to them.

You can also do this by sharing any similar experiences you may have. You can do this only if you have gone through something very similar to what your conversation partner is going through. If a friend is telling you about how their partner cheated on them and you've experienced the same thing, then relating it briefly to convey that you know exactly how they feel can be a good idea, so long as you don't detract the focus from them. If, on the other hand, you've only had a dream that your partner was cheating on you and are in a stable and healthy relationship, then relating that dream to your friend is probably not a good idea. Rather than make them feel seen and understood, such a thing will likely make them feel that they're not being heard or listened to, and that's not a feeling you want to evoke in a friend.

Being observant of the people you're talking to and expressing your observations when it's appropriate can also be an immensely helpful tool. Say you notice someone's eyes brighten when they're talking about a specific topic. That can be something to remark on. Not only that, but it can be a sign that you should steer the conversation toward that topic since it's clearly an area of interest for this person. Alternatively, say you noticed someone's smile falter and posture go rigid when a certain topic came up. Odds are this topic makes them uncomfortable. You don't want to remark on that, but taking the opportunity to steer the conversation away from that topic is a good idea. That way, you'll spare your conversation partner some discomfort and awkwardness, especially if they're not close enough to you to share whatever it is that's bothering them yet.

Being observant of your audience in this manner is something known as flexible conversation (Chantal, 2019). Flexible conversation is a tool that will not only make your interactions with other people go more smoothly but also something that will gain your conversation partner's trust and sympathy. Your efforts will doubtless be appreciated and picked up by them. If you're consistent with this type of behavior, over time, it'll earn you that person's trust, which will encourage them to be more transparent with you. It'll further encourage them to treat you with the same level of empathy you're treating them with.

No matter how flexible and empathetic you are in conversation, none of it will matter much if people can't understand you while you're talking. This is why pacing is so important in conversation. You neither want to talk so slowly that people lose interest or their patience while listening to you nor so quickly that they can't quite make out what you're saying. The speed at which you're talking might seem reasonable to you, but if people look bored while you're talking or if they keep saying things like, "I'm sorry, what was that?", then there is a problem. One way to see if this is the case is to record yourself while talking for a bit. You can then close your eyes and listen to the recording. Can you make out everything you said, or are you going too fast? Are you going at a reasonable pace, or are you taking a lot of unnecessary pauses? One or two pauses here and there aren't necessarily a bad thing, especially if they come at suspenseful moments, like when you're telling a really good story. However, if you're taking pauses between every few words, then you risk boring your audience or losing their attention.

Once you've listened to your recording and identified your pacing issue, you can start working on it. One thing you may notice is that your pacing is particularly thrown off when you get excited about something. A similar thing may happen when you're angry. In such cases, it's important to take an intentional pause to calm down, especially since getting angry may mean saying things you'll regret. One policy you can adopt in arguments, where this might happen often, is to take a break when things are getting heated. You and your conversation partner can use this break to calm down separately and gather your thoughts. Once you have, you can sit down and revisit the discussion more calmly. To make sure you revisit the conversation, set a definitive time for your pauses. That way, you can avoid a situation where you let things lie as they are for too long, thereby leaving matters unresolved and letting unpleasant feelings and thoughts fester.

There's one last thing you can do to become a better communicator overall: You can learn to manage your stress and anxiety. Stress and anxiety, like fear and anger, can cause you to say things you don't mean. They can similarly make you rush into decisions or procrastinate and avoid them. You may find yourself putting off an important conversation with a friend, for example, because you're stressed about it. If that conversation is about a fight you had, doing so won't help you. It'll only make matters worse. Should this situation go on for long enough, it may even do some permanent damage to your relationship. That is a situation you decidedly want to avoid, which you can do if you learn how to manage your stress and anxiety and, thus, prevent them from dictating your thoughts and behaviors.

Chapter 6:

Being a Good Listener

Relationships are about give and take, and part of the "give" entails proper listening. The thing is, there are very few people who know how to listen to others properly. Most people fall into one of two categories: those who don't understand how important listening is and those who think they're good listeners when they aren't. The people who fall into the former category tend to underestimate listening. They think talking is far more important and conclude it's what effective communication is all about, especially if the goal in a given moment is to convince someone of something. The people who fall into the latter category acknowledge that listening is important but don't know how to do it. They think that simply hearing the words that are being said to them—or at least hearing part of them—is enough to be a good listener. It's not. Some years ago, a study was conducted among people who thought they were good listeners. These people were given a speech and then asked what they remembered from it. Most of them were only able to remember 25% of what had been relayed to them, which is a paltry percentage when you think about it (Nichols & Stevens, 2014). The implications this has for work presentations and important meetings are fascinating, if not terrifying, to think about.

While we may have stated that listening is an important part of communication, you may still find yourself asking "Why?" Why is listening to others properly so important? What difference can learning how to listen make in conversation? Can it truly make you a better communicator? Let's see...

Why Listening Matters

We human beings have certain needs. Some of those needs, like sustenance and water, are obvious. Others are less so; but while they may be more subtle, they're no less important. The need to be heard is one such need. As human beings, we have a deep-seated need to be heard because being heard makes us feel validated (*The Importance of Being Heard*, 2022). When you feel validated, you feel that you matter to the person before you. You feel respected by them. Feeling that you are heard, then, makes you feel that your thoughts and feelings are important, have meaning, and are accepted. By extension, feeling that you're validated makes you feel that you truly belong somewhere.

Given all that, making someone feel heard by really listening to them can be a transformative experience for your relationship with them. It can increase the trust they place in you; how open, honest, and transparent they are with you; and how close the two of you are. In other words, genuinely listening to someone is something that can foster your connections with them and make them stronger. At the same time, it can allow you to understand the person before you better. When you truly listen to someone, you get to grasp their perspective, which may be different from your own experiences and emotions. You get to grasp why they act and think the way they do and where they're coming from when they do so, which strengthens your bonds with them even more (Michelitsch, 2023).

Good listening skills aren't only great for your personal relationships, though. They're very helpful for your business relationships and professional settings, too. For instance, good listening skills can make sure that you fully and thoroughly understand a task your manager is giving or a colleague is relaying to you at work. It can ensure you don't miss or forget any vital information or misunderstand anything that's presented to you. This will enable you to do your job and finish your task to the best of your abilities, allowing you to shine at work.

On top of that, proper listening can help resolve conflicts sooner, too, regardless of whether they're personal or professional. A number of the conflicts we have in life stem from misunderstandings, as you may know. Since listening well can reduce the number of misunderstandings that may occur in a conversation, it can also reduce the number of conflicts you get into. Aside from that, your listening skills can help you understand why someone was offended or upset by a certain action or behavior. You can thus come to understand the reason behind a particular argument or fight more quickly and address it. You can apologize for any mistakes you made or clarify a misunderstanding that upset someone. In short, you can get to the root causes of conflicts quickly, thanks to your listening skills, and solve those conflicts before they worsen and spoil everyone's day.

An added benefit is that understanding the root causes of various conflicts can help you avoid them in the future. If you know what kind of behavior is upsetting for someone, for instance, you can avoid it in the future and keep from having an unnecessary argument. This is only possible if you know how to listen, though, since otherwise, you'll let your assumptions, which may be biased, dictate your actions and lead you in the wrong direction, making it impossible for you to avoid similar problems in the future. How can you avoid or solve a problem if you don't know its true cause?

How to Be a Good Listener

As you can see, the question we should be asking, where listening is concerned, isn't "Does it really matter?" It's "How can I be a good listener?" The first thing you need to do to be a good listener is to be open to an actual conversation, where you listen as much as you talk. If you're closed off to a conversation, then it won't matter if you're a good listener or not. Signs that you're closed off from a conversation are that you don't ask people open-ended questions and you don't give proper responses to questions being asked of you. If you respond to open-ended questions by giving monosyllabic answers, then you're undeniably giving the "I don't want to continue this conversation, leave me alone" message. In this case, why would your conversation partner want to keep talking to you?

You can convey that you're open to genuine conversation by using the various methods we covered in the previous chapter. When that is done, you can focus on the task at hand: listening. If you want to get good at listening, you have to learn to get comfortable with the occasional pause and silence (Morrison, 2017). While these may feel a little awkward initially, they're prime opportunities for your conversation partner to start talking and for you to listen. More importantly, pauses and silences give people some added time to reflect on what has been said up to that point. They allow for greater understanding and for both conversation partners to formulate better thought-out, deeper, more meaningful responses. These are responses that you'll be able to listen to carefully and use to obtain more insight about the other person.

Taking advantage of silence in this way goes hand in hand with another tactic you can use, which is to talk less. Rather than rambling on about a subject, keep things short and to the point. Focus on relaying the key message, and then stop talking. Let the person before you have the opportunity to properly respond and elaborate on their thoughts. Pay attention to what they're saying, rather than thinking about what you want to say next or how to respond. Try to understand what they're talking about, even if you don't necessarily agree with them. While you're at it, ask open-ended questions when you can. This will prompt them to elaborate on what they're saying even more, allowing you to listen more closely, not to mention that it will keep the conversation going for longer.

Listening, at its core, is about paying attention to what's being said to you. If you're thinking about what you want to say next when someone is telling you a story, or if you're planning your counterargument while someone is making their case, then you're not paying attention. You're also obviously not paying attention if you're daydreaming or if your mind is wandering off to other matters while someone is talking to you. The same can be said for judging people as they're talking for two reasons. First, when you judge people, you turn your focus away from what they're relaying and toward your judgmental thoughts. Second, when you judge people, you cut off any possibility of understanding their perspective, circumstances, and feelings. You effectively build a wall between you and the person. That wall inevitably reflects on your actions, whether you want it to or not, thereby stymying your conversation partner's efforts to talk to you. Sensing your reticence, they give up trying to share their thoughts and feelings with you. You lose an important opportunity you could have used to foster genuine connection and trust.

There may be times in a conversation when you're unsure of what to say. This is something that can happen to anyone, and there are two ways to handle it. You can either take the opportunity to ask more questions and grasp the situation more so you can respond more thoughtfully and insightfully, or you can respond just to respond. If you go with the former method, you'll deepen the conversation and demonstrate that you are truly paying attention and care about what the person is saying. If you do the latter, you will come across as dismissive and uncaring, even if you are making an effort to understand. Your efforts will not be noticed in this scenario.

There are a number of reasons why you may be unsure of how to respond to someone. The most common reason is that you're unsure what you're supposed to say (Rakshit, 2021). Say a colleague to you has lost someone they care about. As their friend, you want to be there for them, but you're at a loss as to what to say, especially since you're not as close to them as you are to your outside-of-work friends. The words, "I'm sorry for your loss," seem so paltry to you. So, you start stressing. You worry you're going to say the wrong thing, so you either ramble on or don't say anything. Neither of these things is the approach you want to go with because they fail to convey your care and empathy and deny them the opportunity to get things off their chest, which they may need to do at that moment, particularly if they're back to work soon after their loss. What you need to do, on the other hand, is to simply listen and give them the opportunity they need to talk. Say, "I'm here for you," and then simply be there for them. Your work friend will either take the opportunity to talk and share their burden with you, or they'll keep silent, in which case you'll offer your support through your presence. Sometimes, that's all a person needs, and words aren't needed at all and such support can make a work environment much easier to be a part of.

One thing you always want to do when listening to people is to show that you're paying attention to them.

This doesn't mean constantly interrupting them to show that you are. That will have the opposite effect than what you intend. You can easily show you're listening to someone through your body language. Maintaining eye contact while someone is talking to you is a great way of doing this. So is keeping an open, relaxed posture and leaning slightly toward the person who's talking to you. All these measures convey interest and engagement, which make the person before you feel heard and keep talking.

Understanding and listening go hand in hand. However, understanding someone else's feelings and thoughts isn't always the easiest thing to do, particularly if they're different from our own. There's something that can help you when you encounter this situation, which you inevitably will: visualization. If you're having trouble empathizing with someone and grasping what they're trying to tell you, make an effort to visualize their circumstances and situation. Picture whatever it is they're describing in your mind's eye. In the process, try to feel what they're feeling and going through. This method might not work immediately, as it is a slower process than some of the other techniques we've covered so far. However, it's immensely effective because it will make your conversation partner's experiences and feelings more real and tangible for you. It'll make them more relatable.

A second way of making your conversation partner's words more relatable and understandable for you is to ask clarifying questions. Such questions have the power to both demonstrate you're listening and increase your understanding. They can keep misunderstandings to a minimum and help conversations go more smoothly. Conversations will also go more smoothly if you resist the urge to interrupt people. Let's be honest: No one likes being interrupted, as it makes them feel like their words don't matter. Interrupting people is a sure way to show people you don't care about what they have to say. Avoid it as much as possible. It doesn't matter how interesting or important the thing you want to interject with is. If it isn't something that needs to be urgently said—like if there's a fire behind your conversation partner that they need to be made aware of—it can and should wait.

Interrupting someone is not the same as mirroring them, though. Mirroring people is important because it demonstrates you're paying attention. Mirroring people means partially repeating what they've told you to make sure you've understood them correctly. Phrases like "If I understand you correctly..." and "So, you're saying that..." are often used when mirroring people. Mirroring is a great technique to both practice active listening and show you're doing so. The same goes for paying attention to your conversation partner's nonverbal cues, meaning their body language and facial expressions. If you say something that makes your conversation partner cross their arms and take a step back, for instance, odds are you've said something that made them uncomfortable. This could be an important cue to stop and reflect on what you said. If, on the other hand, your conversation partner's smile grew brighter and they leaned in toward you in response to something you said, that's a sure sign they've grown interested. That means you can stick with whatever topic you're discussing and your conversation partner will probably have some interesting things to say about it that you should listen to.

While you're listening to your conversation partner, you should always be conscious of your nonverbal cues. What are your body language and facial expressions saying right now? Do you come across as closed off or open? Do you appear to be engaged or disinterested? As a rule, you want to maintain an open and confident stance, meaning you want your back to be straight, your arms and legs to be uncrossed, and your posture to be relaxed. At the same time, you want to wear a neutral but friendly expression. Smiling slightly never hurt. Such things give the message that you're approachable, interested, and willing to listen, and talking to someone like that is infinitely easier than talking to someone who comes across as the human version of a brick wall.

Chapter 7:

Practicing Empathy and

Compassion

Being a good listener partly means being a highly empathetic person. Empathy is a vital part of communication, but so is compassion. Contrary to what you might think, though, empathy and compassion are not the same thing. Empathy is your awareness of how other people think and feel. It's your ability to put yourself in their shoes and experience what they're experiencing. Compassion is your desire to help someone else after attaining this awareness. Given that, it can be said that empathy and compassion, though linked, generate different emotional reactions. The former sparks understanding. The latter sparks feelings like sympathy or even concern (Cherry, 2023a).

The healthy relationships you form with people you care about require both empathy and compassion. You need empathy to truly understand the people in your life. You need compassion to respond to them emotionally and act on what you're feeling. You need both to forge the healthy, caring, and supportive relationships you want, need, and deserve in your life.

Why You Need Empathy and Compassion

The importance of practicing empathy and compassion when communicating with others cannot be understated. After all, it is the combination of these two things that facilitates mutual bonding. The understanding that empathy creates allows you to draw closer to people. The compassion you feel for what they're experiencing makes you take action to support them. This can mean any number of things, from talking things through with them and letting them cry on your shoulder to giving advice or sitting silently with someone so they don't feel alone. Taking such actions wouldn't be possible without both empathy and compassion.

Truthfully, many things wouldn't be possible without the combination of these two attributes. For instance, there can be no such thing as authenticity in a relationship that's devoid of empathy and compassion. To genuinely support someone, you have to truly understand what they're going through. If you don't, you won't know what you need to do to offer them support. You likely won't be very eager to show them support either, which will reflect in your actions. On top of that, any actions you take to support them will feel inauthentic. Practice empathy and compassion and your actions and words will start carrying a different sort of meaning, one that the person you're talking to will truly appreciate.

This being the case, it shouldn't be surprising to hear that only empathy and compassion can foster trust, warmth, and greater honesty in a relationship. Empathy and compassion can foster trust and honesty because they add authenticity to your words and actions. They show that the care you're displaying for someone is real (Panarella, 2020). They demonstrate that you understand someone and don't judge them for whatever it is they're experiencing, thinking, or feeling. This makes the person you're dealing with feel safe and place their trust in you even more. That, in turn, allows them to comfortably share things with you more, thereby increasing the level of honesty between you. At the same time, the empathy-compassion duo fosters warmth because the care you convey through your actions and words increases the warm feelings others have toward you. The genuine care you have for someone becomes reciprocated, resulting in an even closer relationship.

All in all, then, the empathy-compassion duo increases people's ability to open up. It likewise makes it easier for people to be themselves around you, knowing they will not be judged for it. This makes it easier for them to express their emotions and opinions to you. The trust they place in you increases your tendency to do the same, creating a kind of positive feedback loop in the process.

All of this has certain interesting benefits for you. For one, it makes you less judgmental and more understanding of others. How could that not be the case when empathy enables you to grasp different perspectives without judging them and compassion enables you to respond with care and concern toward others, even when they hold opinions you don't agree with? For another, compassion and empathy increase your self-awareness because they let you see how your words and actions affect those around you more clearly. Having obtained this awareness, you get to see how your positive actions impact the people you care about and lean toward those actions more. Simultaneously, they let you glimpse how your more negative behaviors impact those around you. Your growing compassion then allows you to remedy them, which you typically do.

Empathy and compassion have some interesting ramifications for you in your work life, too. To start, they make you a better team player and make it easier for you to collaborate with others. They do this because they make it possible for you to understand your team members' strengths, weaknesses, and struggles. Having grasped this, you become able to divide your team's various tasks according to everyone's strengths and weaknesses. At the same time, you're able to accommodate people, where appropriate, when they're going through tough situations or difficult circumstances that you can sympathize with, thanks to your compassionate nature.

This naturally helps you create a more productive and harmonious work environment. This also increases everyone's job satisfaction, especially your own. Working in an environment where people can collaborate comfortably, communicate about the struggles they're experiencing, ask for help without fearing they'll be judged for it—an already hard thing to do in a work setting, and feel understood and that they belong is significantly more pleasant than working somewhere where you often feel attacked, judged, and criticized.

How to Practice Empathy and Compassion

It's great that empathy and compassion can help us in all these different ways, but how do we use them to their truest potential? How can we learn to become more compassionate and empathetic? We do so by showing empathy and compassion toward ourselves. Think about it: How can you be understanding and caring toward others if you are unable to be that way to yourself? How can you take the time to understand someone if you can't understand yourself? How can you show true concern for someone and try to support them if you cannot support yourself? The answer to all these questions is: You can't. So, your starting point is to practice self-care as part of your everyday life.

Self-care isn't just about pampering yourself with a home spa day, though that can certainly be a part of it if you want. It's also about accepting yourself as you are and without judgment. That doesn't mean not working on yourself, but it does mean accepting that you are a work in progress, just as we all are. It means making an effort to understand why you are the way you are and why you react to certain things the way you do. It means showing yourself kindness and compassion, especially when you make a mistake or react to something in a way you don't want to react. A great way of doing this is to ask yourself how you'd respond to a friend who acted the way you just did. Odds are, you'd be understanding, patient, and compassionate with them, rather than judgmental and condemning.

Once you've identified how you'd treat a friend in this situation, you can focus on treating yourself the same way. This is going to take some time and practice, but you will get better at it over time, especially if you supplement your efforts with practices like journaling. In due course, you'll find that you're becoming much more understanding and compassionate toward yourself, even as you work to change certain behaviors. This will make it much easier for you to be compassionate and understanding toward other people and serve to better your relationships with them.

Fostering empathy and compassion may seem like a tall order, but it's easier than you'd think, so long as you do one essential thing: practice curiosity. Fostering empathy and compassion requires being curious about others. It necessitates asking the question "Why?" (Selby, 2023). "Why?" is a powerful question because it probes deeper into people's motives, reasonings, feelings, thoughts, and experiences. By asking this question, you often discover that people act the way they do for reasons different from what you had assumed. In other words, you prove your own biases and assumptions wrong. You teach yourself never to make assumptions and learn to always ask more questions, especially when someone does or says something you don't agree with.

Asking "Why?" is a crucial tool to foster empathy and compassion, as is putting yourself in other people's shoes or role-playing. Role-playing is an exercise in imagination. You envision yourself in someone else's place, going through whatever it is they're going through. You adopt their perspective on things and try to feel what they're feeling. This can increase your empathy and compassion levels dramatically, as it allows you to experience others' feelings, thoughts, and hardships firsthand. It can be a challenging habit to get into, particularly if you're new to it. However, the more you do it, the easier it will get until finally, you become a pro at it to the point that understanding someone else's point of view won't take much effort at all.

There are, of course, cases where doing all this will be quite difficult, like when someone holds a vastly different opinion than our own. In such cases, it can be very helpful to remind yourself that we are all human and have our own feelings, troubles, and pain points. Just because someone is troubled by something you'd never be troubled by doesn't mean that that thing doesn't cause them any pain. Reminding yourself of this fact can make it easier for you to land on some sort of compromise when you're dealing with arguments stemming from differences of opinion. Focusing on your similarities with other people in such circumstances can likewise do the same.

Differences of opinion can become barriers to empathy and compassion if you let them. A great way to prevent this from happening is to examine your personal biases regularly. We all like to think that we are purely objective, unbiased individuals. The truth is that we all have certain internalized biases, ones we don't even realize we hold. These biases often color our perception of things, the way we react to various people and situations, and how we judge different circumstances. Given that, our internalized biases can prevent us from fully understanding others and reacting the way we should.

To identify your biases, you have to ask yourself why you think the way you do. You have to ask yourself things like, "Why did I think this thought?", "Where does this belief come from?", and "What evidence, if any, do I have that supports this thought or belief?" You then have to answer such questions honestly and analyze your responses objectively. If you do, you'll discover an array of biases you didn't realize you had. The key to remember as you do this exercise is that having biases doesn't mean you're a bad person. Thinking that it does pushes you to deny that you have biases and, therefore, prevents you from working on them. You can consider biases a byproduct of the society we grow up in. They're beliefs we pick up by observing those around us at a young age and internalize without realizing we're doing so. The good thing is that over time and with effort, we can unlearn our biases.

Questioning your beliefs and thoughts is one way of doing this. Another is to let trusted others question your thoughts and ask for feedback from them. You can then take that feedback and think carefully about it without getting upset or offended by it. Your kneejerk reaction to feedback might be to get angry at it or dismiss it. You shouldn't give in to this urge if you mean to change your biases. Instead, you should take a deep, calming breath and listen to what's being said to you with intent (Acton, 2022). That is the only way you will ever be able to use others' feedback to dismantle your biases.

A final way to increase your capacity to feel empathy and compassion is to allow yourself to be vulnerable with others. You might be hesitant to do this because vulnerability is scary and requires a degree of trust. You could get hurt, after all. The more vulnerable you are with others, though, the more vulnerable they'll be with you. The more vulnerable they are with you, the more you'll understand them. The more you're able to empathize with them and show compassion toward them, the better. This dynamic is a prime example of the reciprocity found in healthy relationships. It's the kind of dynamic that both allows you to be there for others and allows others to be there for you when you need it, which is what healthy, balanced relationships are all about.

Chapter 8:

Owning Your Relationships

Not every relationship can be defined as "healthy," as you know. Some are decidedly unhealthy. You may be averse to cutting people you have unhealthy relationships with from your life, especially if you've known them a long time or if they're blood relatives. However, sometimes you must do so. This doesn't mean you should cut someone off the moment you spot a yellow flag, like the first time they test one of your boundaries. Sometimes, you can talk to people and get them to correct their behavior. However, it does mean that not all relationships are salvageable. More to the point, not all relationships should be.

When a Relationship Isn't Good for You

No relationship on Earth is rosy pink all of the time. The fact is that all relationships have their ups and downs. That fact, however, raises an interesting question: How can you tell a rough patch from an unhealthy relationship? The key indicator that your relationship is a toxic one is you. More specifically, it's how that relationship makes you feel. A healthy relationship makes you happy overall. You may be arguing with your partner, for instance, but whatever negative feelings you're experiencing are specific to that moment. They do not last, nor do they define the entirety of your relationship.

A toxic relationship, on the other hand, is one where you feel unhappy perpetually. This unhappiness isn't confined to one argument or moment but is pervasive. In such cases, you may still love your partner, but you do not feel happy with them. Your relationship no longer feels enjoyable. You find yourself constantly arguing with your partner, even over the smallest things, and maybe even dread seeing them. You would never have these kinds of feelings in a healthy relationship. This makes them a sign of toxic ones.

Toxic relationships can also happen in work environments. Signs that you may have a toxic work relationship are that you

- feel unsupported.

- cannot have a respectful or calm conversation.

- are subjected to a great deal of controlling behaviors, like your every work move being dictated or micromanaged.

- feel the need to constantly lie to your colleague or manager.

- often resent or hold grudges against your colleague or manager.

- usually feel disrespected by your colleague or manager.

- are chronically stressed in your work relationship.

- feel that your needs are always ignored at work.

- have stopped practicing self-care since starting work or getting into this new work relationship (Lamothe & Raypole, 2019).

Now, as you may remember, a toxic relationship isn't necessarily an abusive one. This is an important distinction because you cannot fix an abusive relationship, but you *may* be able to fix a toxic one. Your ability to do this is contingent on a couple of things. First, you and whoever you're in this relationship with—for argument's sake, let's say it's a colleague—need to both accept responsibility and be willing to work on your relationship. If one person is willing to do so and the other is denying there's anything wrong with the relationship, you'll never be able to fix anything. Second, both of you need to be willing to invest your time and energy to change things. In other words, you need to be willing to take action. Third, you need to stop playing the blame game and focus on understanding each other's perspectives instead. You need to start using your empathy skills a bit more.

Having made these three commitments, you can take action to fix your relationship. What if your actions are proving ineffective, though? In that case, you're going to have to take measures to protect yourself. To start, you can have an open, honest, no-frills conversation about how your relationship is affecting you in the hopes that you'll be heard. As part of that conversation, you can set some very firm boundaries. As with any boundary, you'll have to stick with them for them to work.

In some cases, these measures will prove effective. In others, they won't, and you'll find that the other person is trying to cross your new boundaries intentionally. If your colleague does this, an added measure may be to limit the time you spend with them to preserve your mental and emotional health. If you're working closely or on the same projects, this may mean talking to your manager to be reassigned, even if only temporarily. It can mean physically taking breaks from them by going on walks or doing things with your other colleagues, too.

Understandably, you're going to feel a lot of emotions through this process. This is where your support system comes in. You need to talk to your support system, as well as use other methods to decompress, like journaling or perhaps meditating. These practices should help you calm down and better understand what you're going through. As you do these things, you may notice that, unfortunately, nothing is working. Nothing is getting fixed because the other person has no intention of joining you in fixing things. That moment of realization is your cue to walk away. This may be hard to do, but it will be what you have to do if you are to prioritize the most important person in your life: you.

Chapter 9:

Checking In With Each

Other

Having healthy relationships is very important for our mental health because it allows us to get help and support. This is something we're all aware of, so you'd think we'd all be able to easily ask for help from friends and family when we need it. Yet, asking for help isn't always the easiest thing to do. Sometimes, it can be the hardest thing you ever do because it requires being vulnerable with others (Vries, 2023). It requires saying, "I'm struggling with something" and trusting that your friends and family will help you through it. An important word you might have noticed there is "trust." Trust is a must when asking for someone's support. So, consider who you trust most in this life carefully. Who would you trust to be there for you in your time of need? Who would you trust to help you without judging you in any way? Who would you trust to lend you their shoulder to cry on or even cry with you? The people who come to mind as you answer those questions are the people you turn to when you need help. They're also the people you check in with regularly.

What Does "Checking In" Mean?

There can be a lot of reasons why someone is hesitant to ask for help. They might be afraid of being a burden to others. They might be thinking that dealing with things without getting any help is a sign of strength when it really isn't. They might have trust issues or be in denial that the problems they're facing are as bad as they are, just to give a few examples. These reasons can cause people to keep quiet when they should speak out, which is why you should get into the habit of regularly checking in with the people you care about. Checking in on people means asking them how they are doing and not letting them get away with a simple "I'm fine" and leaving it at that. It means probing deeper into how your friends and family are doing and getting them to talk about their lives, how they're currently feeling, and what they're thinking.

Checking in on your colleagues or subordinates is important because it can help you spot when they need help but aren't saying it. It can enable you to be there for them without them having to ask, supply them with what they need, and, consequently, ensure that the work gets done as it's supposed to. It can help you convey that you care about them and want them to be well, even when you happen to be checking in when things are going great for them. In such cases, you'll be able to express how happy you are for them and their well-being and, again, convey how much you care about them.

Though checking in with your loved ones regularly is important, there are times when you should do so more often. These are times when you spot certain warning signs indicating that someone needs help, like

- pulling a disappearing act

- engaging in more self-destructive behaviors

- acting more taciturn and irritable than usual

- engaging in negative, self-defeatist talk (Shrikant, 2023)

Pulling a disappearing act means cutting off contact with the people in your life as much as you can. In other words, it's self-isolation, where you don't call others, go out to meet with people, attend events, or answer texts and calls. This is a major sign that someone needs help but isn't asking for it. So is engaging in self-destructive behaviors. If a friend who didn't use to drink very much is suddenly polishing off a bottle of wine per night, then clearly, they're going through something. The same goes for picking up a smoking habit, binge eating, and any other type of self-destructive behavior.

How about irritability, then? Everyone gets irritable from time to time, like when you miss the last train home late at night. Irritability serves as a sign that something is wrong, not in cases like this, but when it turns into a person's default setting. If a friend of yours is constantly in a bad mood and acting out, then that is a sign that something's wrong, especially if they ordinarily have a sunny personality.

Last but not least, there's self-defeatist talk. Engaging in self-defeatist talk means saying things like "Who would ever want to date me?" or "Of course, I'm not going to get that promotion." If someone is talking to themselves in this way, that's a clear indication that they're not doing well and are mired in negative thoughts. They're so entrenched in them that they've begun to say them out loud to others and have come to consider them irrefutable facts. If that's not a cry for help, I don't know what is.

How to Open Up the Conversation

Say you noticed one of these warning signs in a friend. How are you supposed to check in on them? You begin by asking the right questions. This doesn't mean asking, "How's it going?" and believing your friend when they give you a curt "Fine." It means asking more probing questions. A couple of key examples include:

- How are things going at work?

- How have you been these last few days?

- What's new in your life?

- What's one good and one bad thing that happened this past week?

- Is there anything that's been weighing on your mind lately?

Pay attention to the details your friend gives as they answer such questions. You can then latch onto those details and ask them to elaborate. If they said things were stressful at work, for example, you could ask them why that's the case. You can have them elaborate on the source of their stress and try to get them to talk about it by asking more open-ended and compassionate questions.

One word that should have caught your attention is "compassionate." If you want your friend to open up to you in their time of need, you have to be compassionate and understanding. Your tone of voice will be critical for this, as will the words you choose. Saying things that demonstrate how much you care about them or how you understand what they're feeling, like any frustration or stress they may be experiencing, is a good idea. The mirroring technique will serve you well at this juncture, so will asking clarifying questions.

For these questions to work, you have to ask them when you have time on your hands. If you're asking your friend how they are while waiting for the next subway to come in and have to hop on it in a minute, then that's not the ideal time to get into things. If you do, you'll have to rush through the talk you're having. This won't give your friend an opportunity to answer your questions, and you'll give the impression that you don't care about the actual answer they have to give. It would be much better, then, to check in with friends when you have the time to do so.

There's one last thing you need to remember about check-ins, assuming you want to do them right: They're not one-and-done deals. This goes double for when a friend is giving any warning signs. What you want to do isn't check in once and call it a day but follow up. You want to gently keep probing and reminding your friend that you're here and you care. You want to keep saying things like, "I don't mean to pry, but I'm here for you, always, if you need me." Keep doing this consistently and slowly but surely, your friend will open up to you and ask for your support.

Conclusion

Lao Tzu once said, "Being deeply loved by someone gives you strength while loving someone deeply gives you courage." This quote applies to all sorts of relationships when you think about it, not just to romantic ones, because relationships, at their core, are the source of both our strengths and our bravery, especially as we pursue our goals, ambitions, and dreams. They're a source of strength because they give us the support we need in the hardest of times. They make us feel loved, cared for, and valued. At the same time, they give us the courage we need to be our most vulnerable selves with others. They give us the courage we need to be honest, authentic, open, and trusting. In short, the relationships we get into throughout our lives help us to be the best versions of ourselves, so long as they are healthy.

Healthy relationships can be difficult to form because a great many of us do not know what they're supposed to look like. There is a great deal of misconceptions out there about healthy and balanced relationships, and these misconceptions confuse and mislead people from time to time. Now that you've arrived at the end of *The Book of... Relationship Building*, though, you know exactly what those misconceptions are. You know the kinds of toxic behaviors and patterns these misconceptions can lead to. More importantly, you know exactly what you need to do to avoid them and form healthy relationships that can become your source of strength and bravery.

Now, all you need to do is take that first necessary step to make those relationships a regular, concrete part of your life. There's only one question left to ask yourself: Are you ready to forge the supportive, caring relationships in your life that you need and deserve and shape yourself into the best version you can be?

Note from the Scott

Thank you for taking the time to reading The Book of... Relationship Building, I hope you have enjoyed it and have found at least one thing to help you with your relationships. If you would like to find out more or start a conversation you can connect with me on Linkedin or via my website:

Linkedin Profile: scottdavidsnell

www.inclusive-growth.org

References

A quote by Lao Tzu. (n.d.). GoodReads. https://www.goodreads.com/quotes/2279-being-deeply-loved-by-someone-gives-you-strength-while-loving

Acton, C. (2022, February 4). *Are you aware of your biases?* Harvard Business Review. https://hbr.org/2022/02/are-you-aware-of-your-biases

Antonucci, T. C., Ajrouch, K. J., & Birditt, K. S. (2014). The Convoy Model: Explaining social relations from a multidisciplinary perspective. *The Gerontologist, 54*(1), 82–92. https://doi.org/10.1093/geront/gnt118

Benefits of social relationships. (n.d.). Drink Koia Online. https://drinkkoia.com/blogs/blog/benefits-of-social-relationships

BetterHelp Editorial Team. (2023, October 16). *The importance of communication in a relationship.* BetterHelp. https://www.betterhelp.com/advice/relations/the-importance-of-communication-in-a-relationship

Brant, A. (2023, October 23). *The importance of setting boundaries: 10 benefits for you and your relationships.* BetterHelp. https://www.betterhelp.com/advice/general/the-importance-of-setting-boundaries-10-benefits-for-you-and-your-relationships

Brueck, H. (2023, January 9). *Ditch your toxic relationships — healthy friendships actually help you live longer and heal wounds faster. Here's why.* Insider. https://www.insider.com/good-relationships-help-you-live-longer-reduce-physical-pain-2023-1

Chantal. (2019, April 18). *Key skills for flexible communication.* Absolute Learning. https://www.absolutelearning.co.uk/key-skills-for-flexible-communication

Cherry, K. (2021, April 24). *Why self-esteem is important for success.* Verywell Mind. https://www.verywellmind.com/what-is-self-esteem-2795868#:~:text=Why%20Self%2DEsteem%20Is%20Important

Cherry, K. (2023a, June 5). *Compassion vs. empathy: What's the difference?* Verywell Mind. https://www.verywellmind.com/compassion-vs-empathy-what-s-the-difference-7494906#:~:text=While%20both%20involve%20responding%20to

Cherry, K. (2023b, December 6). *Are your relationships healthy? Here's how to tell.* Verywell Mind.

https://www.verywellmind.com/all-about-healthy-relationship-4774802#toc-characteristics-of-healthy-relationships

Cooks-Campbell, A. (2022, March 10). *Open-ended questions: How to build rapport and be in the know.* BetterUp. https://www.betterup.com/blog/open-ended-questions

Durant, I. (2023, October 5). *How do I keep my tone of voice neutral?* Peep Strategy. https://peepstrategy.com/how-do-i-keep-my-tone-of-voice-neutral

Gould, W. R. (2020, December 8). *What is codependency?* Verywell Mind. https://www.verywellmind.com/what-is-codependency-5072124

Harris, M. (2019, September 26). *Positive relationships boost self-esteem, and vice versa.* American Psychological Association. https://www.apa.org/news/press/releases/2019/09/relationships-self-esteem

How does social connectedness affect health? (2023, March 30). Centers for Disease Control and Prevention. https://www.cdc.gov/emotional-wellbeing/social-connectedness/affect-health.htm

Human characteristics: Social life. (2022, July 7). The Smithsonian Institution's Human Origins Program. https://humanorigins.si.edu/human-

characteristics/social-
life#:~:text=Social%20bonds%20helped%20en
sure%20humans

Hutchinson, J. (2020, April 8). *Transparent communication.*
Michigan State University.
https://workplace.msu.edu/transparent-
communication/#:~:text=At%20a%20Glance-

Kent, R. G., et al. (2015). Social relationships and sleep
quality. *Annals of Behavioral Medicine, 49*(6), 912–
917. https://doi.org/10.1007/s12160-015-
9711-6

Kong, Y. (2022). Are emotions contagious? A
conceptual review of studies in language
education. *Frontiers in Psychology, 13.*
https://doi.org/10.3389/fpsyg.2022.1048105

Koutsimani, P., et al. (2019). The relationship between
burnout, depression, and anxiety: A systematic
review and meta-analysis. *Frontiers in Psychology,
10*(284).
https://doi.org/10.3389/fpsyg.2019.00284

Lamothe, C., & Raypole, C. (2019, November 11). *38
signs of a toxic relationship and tips for fixing it.*
Healthline.
https://www.healthline.com/health/toxic-
relationship#moving-forward

Lawler, M. (2023, March 17). *What is self-care and why is it
critical for your health?* Everyday Health.
https://www.everydayhealth.com/self-care

Lee, K. (2018). *Why is it so hard to set boundaries?* Psychology Today. https://www.psychologytoday.com/us/blog/rethink-your-way-the-good-life/201809/why-is-it-so-hard-set-boundaries

McKay, B.. (2018, August 21). *Talk WITH people, not AT them.* The Art of Manliness. https://www.artofmanliness.com/people/social-skills/talk-with-people-not-at-them

Mehndiratta Kappal, J. (2020, April 30). *Communication skill boosts creativity.* LinkedIn. https://www.linkedin.com/pulse/communication-skill-boosts-creativity-jyoti-mehndiratta-kappal/

Michelitsch, D. (2023, June 4). *The power of listening: How active listening can influence your personality formation.* LinkedIn. https://www.linkedin.com/pulse/power-listening-how-active-can-influence-your-dominik-michelitsch

Morrison, L. (2017, July 18). *The subtle power of uncomfortable silences.* BBC. https://www.bbc.com/worklife/article/20170718-the-subtle-power-of-uncomfortable-silences

Nichols, R. G., & Stevens, L. A. (2014, August). *Listening to people.* Harvard Business Review. https://hbr.org/1957/09/listening-to-people

Panarella, M. (2020, January 24). *Leading with empathy and authenticity.* Forbes.

https://www.forbes.com/sites/forbesbusinessd
evelopmentcouncil/2020/06/24/leading-with-
empathy-and-authenticity/?sh=e10253e580e8

Pattemore, C. (2021, June 3). *10 ways to build and preserve better boundaries.* Psych Central. https://psychcentral.com/lib/10-way-to-build-and-preserve-better-boundaries#10-tips

Rakshit, D. (2021, November 20). *The pressure to always say the "right" thing affects the way we communicate.* The Swaddle. https://www.theswaddle.com/the-pressure-to-always-say-the-right-thing-affects-the-way-we-communicate

Reid, S. (2023, March 1). *Setting healthy boundaries in relationships.* Help Guide. https://www.helpguide.org/articles/relationships-communication/setting-healthy-boundaries-in-relationships.htm

Schroeder, J., et al. (2014, May 29). *Handshaking promotes cooperative dealmaking.* Social Science Research Network. https://doi.org/10.2139/ssrn.2443551

Scott, E. (2020, July 4). *What is a toxic relationship?* Verywell Mind. https://www.verywellmind.com/toxic-relationships-4174665

Selby. (2023, August 21). *Developing empathy: How to strengthen perspective-taking skills.* Everyday Speech. https://everydayspeech.com/sel-implementation/developing-empathy-how-to-strengthen-perspective-taking-skills/#:~:text=Asking%20open%2Dended%20questions%20encourages

Shrikant, A. (2023, April 3). *4 signs you need to check in on your friends, according to a Harvard-trained psychologist.* CNBC. https://www.cnbc.com/2023/04/03/harvard-trained-psychologist-how-to-check-in-on-your-friends.html

Smith, S. (2021, June 23). *The importance of communication in relationships.* Marriage Advice. https://www.marriage.com/advice/communication/importance-of-communication-in-relationships

Suttie, J. (2019, February 1). *Why the world needs an empathy revolution.* Greater Good. https://greatergood.berkeley.edu/article/item/why_the_world_needs_an_empathy_revolution

The health benefits of strong relationships. (2010, November 22). Harvard Health. https://www.health.harvard.edu/staying-healthy/the-health-benefits-of-strong-relationships

The importance of being heard. (2022, September 28). The DMC Clinic. https://thedmcclinic.ie/blog-the-importance-of-being-heard

Thompson, J. (2011, September 30). *Is nonverbal communication a numbers game?* Psychology Today.

https://www.psychologytoday.com/us/blog/b
eyond-words/201109/is-nonverbal-
communication-a-numbers-game

Tolstoy, L. (2008). *Anna Karenina*. Pearson Education.
(Original work published 1877)

Vries, M. F. R. K. de. (2023, July 1). *Why it's so hard to
ask for help?* Harvard Business Review.
https://hbr.org/2023/07/why-its-so-hard-to-
ask-for-
help#:~:text=The%20fear%20of%20being%20
vulnerable

Wool, M. (2021, July 29). *Talk less, listen more: 6 reasons it
pays to learn the art.* BetterUp.
https://www.betterup.com/blog/talk-less-
listen-more

Yang, Y. C., et al. (2016). Social relationships and
physiological determinants of longevity across
the human life span. *Proceedings of the National
Academy of Sciences*, *113*(3), 578–583.
https://doi.org/10.1073/pnas.1511085112

Yi Wong, G. (2021, March 2). *3 simple ways to express
empathy in your next conversation.* Ideas Ted.
https://ideas.ted.com/4-easy-ways-to-express-
empathy-in-your-next-conversation